ORGANISED FUN

About the Author

Josie Curran is thirty-two years old and lives in a houseboat on an island in the Thames with her boyfriend, Barney, their dog and a gathering of adopted wildfowl. When she's not mucking about on beaches, campsites or under dinner tables, Josie works as a fundraiser for Kids Company, assisting Camila Batmanghelidjh in her work with underprivileged children.

ORGANISED FUN

**A treasure trove of games
and tomfoolery**

Josie Curran

BOXTREE

First published 2009 by Boxtree
an imprint of Pan Macmillan Ltd
Pan Macmillan, 20 New Wharf Road, London N1 9RR
Basingstoke and Oxford
Associated companies throughout the world
www.panmacmillan.com

ISBN 978 0 75222 710 8

A CIP catalogue record for this book is available from
the British Library.

Designed and typeset by Ben Cracknell Studios

Printed in the UK by CPI Mackays, Chatham ME5 8TD

Visit **www.panmacmillan.com** to read more about all our books
and to buy them. You will also find features, author interviews and
news of any author events, and you can sign up for e-newsletters
so that you're always first to hear about our new releases.

Contents

This book is dedicated to the memory of
my dearest friend and grandmother,
Elizabeth Stranger Holman.

Introduction

'We do not stop playing because we grow old,
we grow old because we stop playing.'

Benjamin Franklin

The suggestion of playing a game will divide any room in two quicker than the Marmite debate. There are those who leap gleefully from their seats with suggestions and pointy elbows and others who hide behind cushions quaking at the potential humiliation.

Once everyone has been bullied into submission, the next hurdle game players always face is one of memory. It starts with the inevitable quandary of which game to play, extending into a parliamentary session on how to play it. You can be pretty sure that your brother can't really remember the details of the game that Simon with the dreadlocks showed him on the beach in Phuket, and inevitably everyone groans as Uncle Barry gets his way and you all end up playing Charades for the fifteenth consecutive year. Don't get me wrong, I'm not knocking a classic, but everyone needs variety.

When it comes to games, I probably fall into the pointy-elbow category. As a feral child with three siblings who ran amok in my aunt's field, my memories abound with homespun fun. From sailing cardboard boxes across the lawn to husky-racing my sisters down the lane, my garden dictatorship meant my siblings were always on hand to facilitate my entertainment plans. University was probably where this really blossomed. I remember spending much of this crucial academic time leading nightclub dance floors to aerobic routines, and there was always a demand for developing novel ways to fill lecture-free hours.

That is why I've written this book: to put an end to the days of, 'How does that game go again?' and to provide a spot of inspiration as to the wealth of game-playing ideas out there, if only to prevent Uncle Barry truly killing off organised fun for future generations. After all, the family that plays together stays together. It's a reminder of how the Victorians had it right. It's both stimulating and fun to entertain ourselves just by talking, adopting strange poses and co-opting household items for props.

Herein lies the beauty of organising your own fun: it's free. In these frugal times, homespun fun definitely receives a gold star from the thrifty-living contingent. Our dependence on television, cinemas and computers has meant we've forgotten that we're also capable of doing the job ourselves. Before you know it, there will be cries of, 'Who needs a television when we have ourselves?', as fears and insecurities disappear and everyone remembers how much they enjoy a spot of organised fun.

A Potted History of Organised Fun

The enduring appeal of games can be traced back through time. Our innate ability to entertain ourselves has provided a rich tapestry of historical frivolity. It's this desire to engage our brains with purposeless diversions that stands us apart from the animal world.

The classical era was a period rich with game-playing heroes. The ancient Egyptians were among the earliest recorded gamers (1). My favourite from their repertoire involves spinning your friends around to create a human whirligig before collapsing in a heaving heap (see Human Whirligig in Chapter Three: Organised Fun for the Beach or Campsite, for full game details). This glittering civilisation of mystery and power was also the inventor of Leapfrog and an early form of Skittles, both represented in finds from recent archaeological digs.

The ancient Greeks were powerhouses of competitive spirit. At the esteemed Greek Games, heroic contenders would demonstrate speed and strength in Chariot Racing or Boxing, while the scholarly pitted their wits against rivals in poetry and philosophical duels.

Then there were the Romans, who were the consummate pioneers of organised fun, with their gladiatorial battles and prestigious games famed for delivering entertainment on a Goliath scale (2). The Romans were also the demons of the board game. These avid stonemasons left rich architectural finds of game boards carved into doorsteps and floors, and even into the bench of an amphitheatre. There must have been a lot of hanging about, trying the patience of game-lovers who were waiting for a favourite slave to enter the pit as lion food.

If you managed to avoid the torture, hangings and witch-burnings that were meted out to allegedly dodgy individuals, life in the age of chivalry was also one rollercoaster of fun. Wealthy children in medieval times were blessed with an impressive toy box. From skipping ropes and rattles to kites and spinning tops, these dandies were never short of ludic diversions. Sadly, such objects of delight were confined to the rich kids. If you were a lucky peasant child, you might be flung a dead baby chick to play with, but only if you were past the age of five and had impressed your parents with surviving so long.

Fortunately, these peasant kids were a tenacious bunch and were able to style their own fun without the need for gimmicky equipment. Stick Fencing (see Chapter One: Organised Fun for the Great Outdoors) and Piggy Back Fighting provided popular distraction, while the more earnest favoured a game of Let's Pretend to Plough the Field with This Stick (3).

The Middle Ages was a period polarised by the feudal system, but widely prone to disease – and to outbursts of wild pleasure seeking. While the ruling classes filled their time with hunting, fishing and drunken orgies (no change there), the peasantry indulged in an early form of football, gambling games and cockfighting. As the towns of Europe thronged with jongleurs, mime troupes and troubadours, closer to home a constant battle simmered between Church and people over the immorality of recreational pursuits, with ecclesiastics condemning any such frivolity as the work of the Devil.

In 1560, Pieter Breugel painted a magical world of games and tomfoolery devoid of adults and named it simply *Children's Games*. The painting swarms with children engrossed in a variety of gaieties and provides a bountiful insight into the games and pastimes of the sixteenth century. One group plays a game of Trip-Up, where a long line of pairs waggle their legs in the air for their friends to pilot through; another shows a trio racing with a small child carried in a seat created from their hands; and a further depicts a novel game of war where two teams of two mounted on each other's backs pull on a circle of rope to dismount their rival.

Fun wasn't confined to the kids in Tudor times, however, with games for grown-ups becoming ever more organised. Festivals were an antidote to a period rigid with discipline and social control. From Midsummer's Day celebrations to the birthday of the village patron saint, it didn't take much to get the Tudor dandy reaching for his glad rags. Such events were embraced at every opportunity, offering a wealth of outlets for lighthearted play and hedonistic giddiness. There would be Bowls and Skittles, Leapfrog and Blind Man's Buff, High Jump and Long Jump, as the cities turned themselves into Meccas of indulgence and excess (4).

The eighteenth century saw the Church's influence settle into the homes of the masses. In this era of high morality, entertainment was permitted as long as it had an educational or moral objective. The jigsaw puzzle, invented during this time, was a reflection of a period of great British exploration and discovery. It featured newly drawn maps and was used to teach the geography of recently discovered worlds. Other board games were created by dominant Protestant publishers, whose teachings focused on reward for goodness and condemnation of evil. One published in 1818 is the snappily entitled *The New Game of Virtue Rewarded and Vice Punished, for the Amusement of Youth of Both Sexes* (5) – it sort of trips off the tongue, doesn't it?

However, it is the Victorians who can be credited for shaping the modern-day format of organised fun among family and friends. The Industrial Revolution saw the emergence of a generation of young men and women who were better off than their ancestors. With so much time on their hands they invented an impressive collection of indoor or 'parlour' games to amuse themselves at intimate gatherings.

It's hard to associate the stiff-upper-lipped Victorians with such revelry, but many of their kooky inventions have lasted through to today. Even with the arrival of the radio and television supposedly marking the near death of self-made fun, these inanities are what people still recall fondly from childhood. Almost everyone has been cajoled into a game of Charades, and Squeak Piggy Squeak has endured as a top-ten children's party favourite.

But the Victorians can't take all the credit for the games that grace the drawing rooms, dinner tables and gardens of today. Generations of families and friends have continued to invent, develop and adapt their own ideas for tomfoolery and fun. From the downright daft to the thoroughly entertaining, homespun fun will always be a unique way to connect us and remind us of our kinship bonds.

Over time, like playing a game of Chinese Whispers, these games have been adapted and refined, tweaked and personalised, to create a diverse and fascinating collection that is in part presented in this book.

How to Use This Book

This book has been structured in such a way that whatever you're up to, you can easily find your way to some ideas and inspiration for creating your own entertainment. The games have been presented in the same format throughout to allow you to quickly grasp the idea and get you stuck into organising some fun.

A word of warning: some of the games in this book could be regarded as a little bit dangerous. Players and parents are advised to exercise caution. In this crazy, nanny-state world, all games are played at your own risk.

Warnings aside, I hope you find the book as much fun to read as the games are to play.

ONE

Organised Fun for the Great Outdoors

I'm one of those rather frustrating people who embrace the great outdoors whatever the weather. You can often find me striding out heartily on a country walk as the hail draws blood across my cheeks and my extremities begin to frost over. It's not to everyone's taste, but I'm a staunch believer that if you get out there, the world isn't as cold as it looks from the kitchen window. A muddy field or sodden woodland can in fact offer a veritable playground of pleasure.

Frolf, or Gisbee

What's the game?

Some friends devised this game while on a long walk through the Monmouthshire countryside. They thought they'd stumbled on a way to bring golf into the twenty-first century, but soon found it to be a recognised sport in the United States. It's a great way to provide added entertainment to a long walk and requires nothing more than a frisbee and some friends.

If you don't have a frisbee to hand, you can always use a round plastic lid or even a sun-dried cowpat (see the end of this chapter for Ultimate Cowpat Frisbee).

What do I need to play it?

One frisbee per player, some friends and a large area to play in. If you're getting serious about it, you could craft some large, chain-like hoops to mark the holes around the course, as they do in the States.

How many friends?

As many or as few as you like.

How do I play it?

- Each player takes it in turn to pick a marker to be the next Frolf target on the course. Before taking a shot at each target, players must agree on the par (a realistic number of throws that it will take to reach that tree, bush or bin). For example, if you agree a par of three and reach the target in two throws, you are one under par.

- The objective of the game is to travel around the course to each target in the smallest number of throws. The winner is the player with the fewest total throws.

Fruit Croquet

What's the game?

A blissful, bizarre way to spend an afternoon. There's a certain art to directing a croquet ball using only a stuffed stocking swinging majestically between your legs. You'll be pleased to hear that it looks every bit as rude and ridiculous as it sounds.

What do I need to play it?

A stocking and an apple or orange for each player. You also need something lighter to be the ball. A tennis ball or a light football is ideal. Finally, you need something to create hoops or mini-goalposts with. We've always used pebbles to mark them, but if you've got some time you can create large hoops by bending garden wire into shape and sticking them in the ground.

How many friends?

A minimum of two and a maximum of eight per game to prevent it going on too long.

How do I play it?

- Each player creates their own croquet 'mallet' by putting a piece of fruit in a stocking and then dangling it between their legs by attaching it to their belt.

- Hands are not allowed, and players must swing their hips to create a pendulum-like momentum which propels the ball towards the hoops.

- Mark out the route by creating hoops or mini-goals around your designated pitch – ideally five or six hoops. You can use pebbles to mark out the hoops, or you can create garden wire hoops as described above.

- Players then play Croquet following the traditional rules. In summary, the object of the game is to get the ball through the appropriate sequence of hoops. Players take it in turns to hit the ball around the course. You only get one go at hitting the ball, unless you go through a hoop and then you get an extra go. If you 'roquet' another player (if you hit their ball with yours), you also get another go. You can only roquet your fellow players' balls once in between each hoop.

Human Croquet

What's the game?

Another novel alternative to the traditional game of Croquet, without the fuss and bother of getting the proper kit. This time the game is played blindfolded, with players adopting the role of the mallet, ball and hoop.

What do I need to play it?

The only equipment you need for this game is people. To make it work properly you actually need quite a few friends – erm, twenty-two, in fact.

How many friends?

Ideally you need twenty-two players: ten pairs to be the hoops, one for the ball and another to be the 'mallet'. It is workable with far fewer players, it just means a lot of running around: those who are the hoops have to manoeuvre themselves into a different position once their hoop has been cleared.

How do I play it?

- Ten pairs of people position themselves around the course facing each other, with their arms raised in the air, clasping each other's hands to create a 'hoop'. If you're playing the game with fewer people, just ask hoop players to move themselves into another position once their hoop has been cleared.

- The 'ball' is then blindfolded and their partner, the mallet, must direct the blindfolded ball through the ten hoops in sequence.

- The mallet moves the ball by standing behind them, turning them in the intended direction, then saying 'Go!'; no further commands can then be given (or contact made) except for a 'Stop!' command.

- Teams take it in turns to play and the usual Croquet rules can apply (see Fruit Croquet above for full details). If you get your ball through a hoop in one go (i.e. from 'Go!' to 'Stop!'), you get another turn. If your ball hits an opponent's, they stay where they are while you get another go. If your ball hits the hoop your go ends and it's the turn of the next player.

- The goal of the game is to get through the hoops in the right sequential order. The first team to make it around the course wins.

Chipping Campden's Olympick Shin Kicking

What's the game?

Chipping Campden is a small village in the Cotswolds that's been hosting its 'Olympick Games' since 1612. The games provide a colourful and eccentric vision of traditional England, with Punch and Judy shows, sword fighting and an array of comedy sporting events.

Shin Kicking is one of the highlights of the games. In the early nineteenth century the activity became rather brutal, with contestants hardening shins with coal hammers and wearing boots tipped with iron to outdo their rivals. If played without too much violence, it provides as much entertainment for viewers as it does for the players.

What do I need to play it?

Some friends with strong shins, and some straw or something similar for padding.

How many friends?

As many as you like.

How do I play it?

- Contestants hold each other by the shoulder and try to kick the shins of their opponents to bring them to the ground.
- The champion is the winner of the best of three challenges in the final bout, having kicked their way successfully through the early rounds.
- A 'stickler', the original name for the Olympick judge, makes sure that shins are hit before a fall can count.
- NB: A note on bruise prevention. Game rules allow for shin protection using straw or similar padding. I'd also recommend a good dose of arnica cream as a post-game treatment to prevent a blossom of bruises on your shins.

The Great Outdoors

Frozen T-Shirt Competition

What's the game?

Definitely one for the summer. This game involves racing to be the first to put on a frozen T-shirt.

What do I need to play it?

A T-shirt for every player and a freezer to prepare them in.

How many friends?

As many as you like.

How do I play it?

- T-shirts are thoroughly soaked the day before and either screwed up and tied into a tight ball or folded up as if to be put away. They are then placed in the freezer overnight. The more water left in the T-shirt the harder it is to put on, so it's up to you whether you want to wring it out or not.

- Players line up with the frozen T-shirts on the floor in front of them. On the signal, players race to put their T-shirts on.

- The first to get their T-shirt all the way on wins.

Gate Vaulting

What's the game?

A long country walk can be made far more interesting when turned into an equestrian-style event. Contestants are awarded points for creativity in clearing gates, fences and stiles. Young, lithe urbanites have been jumping on the bandwagon of this game and can be found hurling themselves over buildings (well, small walls at least) and running up lamp posts across the city streets of the world. Parkour is a sport that's exploded in popularity among the energetic youth and has even been immortalised in the James Bond film *Casino Royale*.

What do I need to play it?

An athletic disposition and sporty footwear are both an advantage.

How many friends?

Can easily be played on your own, though an element of competition with a friend makes it far more entertaining.

How do I play it?

This one needs very little explanation. While on a country walk, players are awarded points for their creativity in clearing whatever obstacles they come across. Some jumping styles and high-scoring suggestions are shown opposite. The person with the most points wins.

The Classic Flip

The Rabbit

The Gymnast

The Cachango

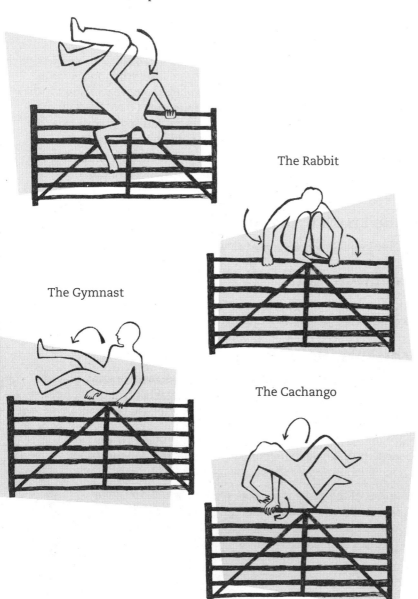

Broom Polo

What's the game?

As a horse-loving, city-living kid I spent much of my childhood cycling around car parks on my trusty rusty bike, imagining it was a noble chestnut steed galloping through the countryside.

After coming across the game of Polo in one of my well-worn pony books, my bike–horse game was soon adapted to include our kitchen broom and I persuaded my younger sisters to join me in a game of Broom Polo. We revisited it as adults one gin-soaked summer afternoon and it proved to hold its magic.

What do I need to play it?

A ball, a bike and a broom per player, with tin cans for goalposts.

How many friends?

You can play it with two of you, but two teams of four (as in a real game of Polo) is the ideal scenario.

How do I play it?

- If there are more than two of you, get yourselves into teams.
- Players mount their bikes and grasp the broom as if it were a polo mallet, with the sweeping end used to hit the ball.
- Each 'chukka' (period of play) lasts seven minutes and you can choose to play between four and seven chukkas, depending on how much time you've got.
- The object of the game is to score goals to win. Hitting the ball across the line with your broom scores goals. If a ball is knocked by your bike rather than your broom, this is also counted as a goal.
- The team with the most goals at the end of the chukkas wins.

The Great Outdoors

Cow Sniffing

What's the game?

Much to my mother's fear and loathing, my three siblings and I used to play this the minute we arrived at our aunt's house in Devon. Please play with caution and it's totally at your own risk. You've been warned.

What do I need to play it?

A field full of cows.

How many friends?

As many or as few as you like.

How do I play it?

- Find a field of cows. Make sure there are no bulls or bullocks (baby bulls) in there. Young heifers (female cows) are the best as they're intensely curious without the bullishness of the male variety.

- Lie down next to each other, or on your own if you're playing solo, in a cowpat-free area and close your eyes.

- The natural curiosity of a cow means that within a few minutes (or hours, if it's a hot, lazy day) you will attract the attention of the majority of the herd.

- You must now lie as still and quiet as possible. The player who is brave enough to lie there the longest while twenty dewy slimy muzzles are pushed in their face wins.

- The perceived saving grace of the game is that the minute someone moves, the herd scatters – hopefully away from you.

Easter Lindt Bunny Lamping

What's the game?

We invented this one Easter at a friend's house in Wales. It's best played with those gold foil-wrapped Lindt bunnies, though anything with a reflective surface works just as well. Kids love it and it's a great way to make a traditional Easter-egg hunt a lot more exciting.

For those not versed in the ways of the country, bunny lamping is a method that's used to catch rabbits to keep populations in check. Hunters go out with torches and shine them into rabbit-infested areas. When the light hits a rabbit, their eyes light up like bulbs, similar to when they're caught in car headlights.

What do I need to play it?

A strong torch and some foil-wrapped chocolate treats – the larger the better – and at least one for every player. Oh, and a night sky.

How many friends?

This requires at least one person to plan and manage the game and as few or as many as you like to play it.

How do I play it?

The organiser needs to go into the garden or on a well-known walk when it's still light, and strategically hide the foil-wrapped goodies in positions where they'll shine when the torchlight hits them.

Next, write a set of creative clues to mark out the trail. You might want to be cryptic about it, for example if the foil-wrapped chocolates are hidden in the daffodils, your clue might allude to Wordsworth's famous poem. Alternatively, and especially if you're playing with young kids, you can be fairly literal, for example the clue might read: 'Under a heavy green object ten paces from the front door.'

When everything is set up and it's dark enough outside, hand a copy of the clues to each of the hunters, who then compete to find the foil-wrapped treasure by shining their torches around the directed area until a burst of gold flashes out.

Tin Can Horseshoes

What's the game?

This is a traditional English village game honed by the young farmers of Britain. As horseshoes aren't found in abundance in the city, you can also play using empty tin cans or anything that has a ring-like shape.

What do I need to play it?

For the traditional game, you'll need horseshoes and a metal or wooden stake (or even a sturdy stick) that can be firmly hammered into the ground. If not easily accessible, then clean out some old tin cans and open at both ends. The standard 400g tin cans are in fact pretty tricky to loop over so you might want to use the wider ones or even manufacture yourself a ring using rope or string.

How many friends?

As many or as few of you as you like.

How do I play it?

- Get yourself set up by hammering a stake into the ground.
- The object of the game is to get your horseshoe or tin can over the stake.
- Players have three shots to try to hoop it over the stake in the ground to win a prize.

Tug of War

What's the game?

For those whose childhood isn't blemished with memories of a village fête, a Tug of War is where people split into two teams and demonstrate their superior strength by yanking each other over a line on the ground.

What do I need to play it?

A very long piece of rope and a handkerchief, though if you decide to do it Egyptian-style, i.e. by pulling on each other's hands, then no equipment is necessary.

How many friends?

A minimum of two, or as many as you like.

How do I play it?

- Split into two teams, ideally with someone acting as the umpire.
- The umpire makes a mark in the ground and ties the handkerchief around the middle of the rope. The rope is then placed on the ground with the handkerchief laid over the line.
- The two teams go to either end of the rope and get in line behind each other, each holding the rope firmly.
- On the judge's signal, contestants 'Take up the strain!' and on the next bellow of 'Pull!' the challenge begins.
- The winning team is the one who drags their opponents across the line.
- I've also seen it played across a stream where the losing team get dragged into the water. The prospect of sitting in cold water on losing the contest might hinder your recruitment ability, so I'd suggest keeping it as an option to cool down an overly testosterone-charged crowd.

Emily's Foraging Game, or the Scavenger Hunt

What's the game?

This is my dear friend Emily's favourite game which involves sending your friends out into the forest, garden or patio in a race to find all the nature items on the game list. We once played it when a friend brought his new girlfriend along to meet us all. Her true colours were quick to come to light when she literally pushed one of the other players over to reach a mushroom that was growing in the undergrowth. I think the relationship ended soon after.

As entertaining for adults as it is for kids, it's particularly brilliant for persuading reluctant young walkers that there's more to a country walk than dragging your feet.

What do I need to play it?

A pen and a piece of paper for each team.

How many friends?

As many or as few as you've got.

How do I play it?

- Players choose to play individually or in teams.

- Each team is given a matching list of natural finds or other landmarks that they're likely to come across on their walk. You might choose to put an oak leaf or a lichen-covered twig on your list. Alternatively, depending on the location of your walk, you may opt for a more urban-themed list which involves collecting beer mats from specific pubs or camera-phone pictures of road signs or markings found on your amble.

- The first team back with a completed list wins.

- An extra layer of competition can be added by scoring items depending on how hard they'll be to find.

Schnitzeljagd

What's the game?

This is a popular German variation of the Scavenger Hunt (see page 21). Great to instigate when you're setting off on a country stomp but you are at that rather frustrating stage when half the group is still faffing around making sure their hairclip matches their wellies. Those who are ready can set off on their merry way, leaving a trail for the others to follow.

What do I need to play it?

Stones, sticks and other bits of nature that can be used to mark a trail.

How many friends?

At least two of you – the 'hunter' and the 'hunted' – though bigger teams make it more fun.

How do I play it?

- Before you start, agree on where the game will finish, and ensure the hunted have a collection of sticks, pebbles and chalk to leave their trail.

- Split into two groups, with the hunters being slightly larger in number. The object of the game is for the hunted to reach the designated place before they're caught.

- The hunted are obliged to leave clues along their way to lead and mislead the hunters. The clues must always lead the right way, but you can set false routes as long as they end in a clearly marked X. A selection of other signals are:

    Directional arrow made out of twigs.

    A star of twig arrows to show different possible directions (false and true).

    A chalked X on a tree.

A ribbon tied to a tree to show you're on the right route.

- If the hunted reach the designated point before being found then they're the winners. If the hunters find them before, then they become the winning team.

Slurry Worry

What's the game?

It's amazing how the simple things in life can entertain you for hours. This game came out of last New Year's Eve when we spent the evening at a hog roast field party in an idyllic Cotswold valley. The evening was marked with campfires, guitars and some terrible singing. As the ground got increasingly muddy we came up with this game as a way to get out of the mud.

What do I need to play it?

A muddy field and a long log or fence post laid down flat in the mud.

How many friends?

As many or as few as will fit on the log.

How do I play it?

- Ideally you'll have one player per log, but you can play with multiple players on a long one.

- The object of the game is to stay balanced standing on a log while it sits in a muddy, slurried field. Depending on the consistency of the mud, it can be a lot harder than it sounds.

- On the word 'Go!' players mount their logs and try to balance on top as the log swims and slips in the mud.

- Last man standing wins.

Splat the Rat

What's the game?

This used to be a staple of any country fair. Probably because my attendance at such quintessentially English occasions has dwindled, I haven't seen it in action for years. It requires a bit of preparation but the reusability of the equipment makes it worth the invested time.

What do I need to play it?

A toy rat, a long tube or piece of drainpipe, a plank, something to fix the two together (such as gaffer tape), a stepladder, and a rolling pin or rounders bat to do the splatting.

How many friends?

However many you like.

How do I play it?

- First of all, you need to manufacture your apparatus. Take a long tube about two metres in length – a piece of drainpipe is ideal – and a slightly longer plank of wood, and strap the two together using gaffer tape or similar.

- You need to ensure that the edge of the plank of wood and the drainpipe are aligned and that there's an extra length of wood extending beyond the end of the drainpipe – around 50 centimetres is ideal. This is to provide a 'splatting' area for when the rat shoots out the end of the tube. You then need to set your game up by resting the plank, with the pipe on top, on your stepladder.

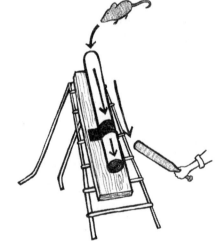

- Once set up and ready to go, the first player positions themselves kneeling down at the bottom of the pipe with the rolling pin gripped in hand.

- The toy rat is then sent scuttling down the tube and the player scores a point if they manage to hit the rat with the rolling pin when it comes out the other end.

Walkie Talkie

What's the game?

My boyfriend and I enjoyed this one on a recent wet and rainy holiday in Wales. As the storm clouds and sheet rain were obscuring any pleasure that could be taken from our scenic coastal walk, we decided to entertain ourselves. It's essentially Consequences (see Chapter Four: After-Dinner Organised Fun: Short Games), but you use your voice instead of pen and paper.

What do I need to play it?

Imagination is a considerable advantage.

How many friends?

At least two of you.

How do I play it?

- Each player takes it in turn to create their own sentence or chapter that builds on the previous idea.

- Slowly a story is constructed, inspired by combined ideas and thinking.

Pooh Sticks

What's the game?

Pooh Sticks were a much-anticipated feature of my childhood holidays in Devon. There's a small stone bridge over the river in the bottom field that we used to hang over to play. We spent hours assessing the water for the fastest flow, nudging each other along to get the prized spot as we steered ourselves for the 'off'.

Pooh Sticks originated from A. A. Milne's tales of Winnie the Pooh. The game can be found in *The House at Pooh Corner* when Christopher Robin and Pooh play on a bridge, throwing fir cones in the water.

Ever since the publication of Milne's book in the early 1900s, the endearing magic of the game has ensured it is passed on through generations. Its popularity is such that since 1984 a World Pooh Sticks Championship has been held at Day's Lock in Oxfordshire each year.

What do I need to play it?

A river with a bridge and some sticks or similar items that you might find lying around.

How many friends?

As many as will fit on your bridge.

How do I play it?

- Players hunt out their chosen stick and memorise what it looks like.

- Next, players must all position themselves along the side of the bridge with the water flowing towards them.

- On the word, everyone drops their sticks into the water, turns and races to the other side to see whose gets there first.

Stick Fencing

What's the game?

Popular with children in medieval times, Stick Fencing provided a thoroughly satisfactory means of entertainment using equipment that could be fashioned from the family apple tree. Quite simply: fencing rules played with sticks.

What do I need to play it?

Sticks – one per player.

How many friends?

A minimum of two or as many as you like.

How do I play it?

- A line is drawn in the ground and the duelling pair take their weapons.

- Each 'bout' consists of three rounds of three minutes each, with a minute's rest in between each round.

- To score a hit, players must battle through the stick defences to achieve a not-too-aggressive touch on their opponent's torso or body zone (which is essentially anywhere from the base of the neck to the hips). Any touch outside this is an invalid hit.

- The winner is the 'fencer' who scores five valid hits.

- If there are a few of you, it makes sense to engage in a bout of team fencing. Get into teams of three and play as before, following the same rules. This time you collectively accumulate your scores. The winning team is the first to an agreed number of hits.

Wally (Pronounced Wall-ee)

What's the game?

Any boy who's spent time at an English secondary school should know this game. Its simplicity and ability to include big groups of kids means it's been rolled out in school playgrounds across the country for years.

What do I need to play it?

A football or a tennis ball and a wall to kick it against.

How many friends?

You can start off small but it works brilliantly for groups of all sizes.

How do I play it?

- If using a tennis ball you can play with your hands or even a tennis racket. If you're playing with a football use your feet.
- Choose a wall that's ideally around two metres high.
- The first player hits or kicks the ball towards the wall, ensuring that it bounces once before bouncing back off the wall. As soon as a player has had their turn, the next player steps forward to take their turn just as the ball bounces back.
- A player is out if they fail to hit or kick the ball when it returns to them, if they fail to make it bounce before hitting the wall or if they miss the wall entirely. The winner is the last person left in.

The Flowerpot Race

What's the game?

This is harder to explain than it is to play. It's a race to the finish line via two flowerpot stepping stones that you move forward on. Confused? Read on.

What do I need to play it?

Two terracotta flowerpots per contestant, or old paint tins are a great alternative. They need to be substantial and strong enough to stand on.

How many friends?

Enough of you to make it a race.

How do I play it?

- A start and a finish line are marked out. If you're particularly organised, you can mark a course around the garden.

- Contestants turn their flowerpots upside down and then use them as stepping stones to race to the finish line. Contestants begin by standing on one flowerpot behind the start line. When the race begins, they each place their second flowerpots in front of them and step onto them, before moving their first flowerpots in front and stepping onto them, and so on.

- The first person to the finish line wins. If you fall off or touch the ground at all you have to go back to the beginning and start all over again.

The Slow Cycling Race

What's the game?

A bicycle race around a designated course without touching the ground. The last one across the finish line wins, which means you have to do it as slowly as possible. If you put your foot on the ground or fall off then you're out.

Last Bike Standing

What's the game?

My neighbour Gareth, who lives in the houseboat opposite, told me about this one. He and some friends came up with it while on a camping trip. It's an adaptation of the Slow Cycling Race but involves players trying to force their opponents to put their feet on the ground.

What do I need to play it?

A bike per player.

How many friends?

You can play it with two, but it's more fun with three or four.

How do I play it?

- First of all, agree the boundaries of the cycle area.

- The objective of the game is to be the last bike standing. Players are out as soon as they put their feet on the ground.

- To play, players cycle around, trying to block each other's paths, forcing their opponents to put their feet on the ground.

- No pushing, hitting or gouging allowed. But other non-violent, non-sportsmanlike tactics are encouraged.

Duck Roulette

What's the game?

The flotilla of feathered friends who share our stretch of the Thames all have names. There are Marvin and Amanda the mandarins, James and Arcadia the white swans and Jerry and Terry the gay mallards who hang out in the bush in our garden.

My boyfriend Barney and our friend Ollie came up with this to provide a focus to the regular duck-feeding frenzy that happens in front of our boat each morning.

What do I need to play it?

Some ducks, geese or swans. You need at least ten of them to make it a decent game.

How many friends?

You could play it on your own but having a friend with you makes it much more fun.

How do I play it?

- This game is best played with a large group of ducks.
- The objective of the game is to successfully feed the duck you pick out from the group.
- First of all, pick your duck. You must now throw your duck-food item to the duck that you've named.
- If your nominated duck eats your piece of bread, you get a point.

Wife Carrying

What's the game?

Wife Carrying dates back to the early nineteenth century but has been an official sport in Finland since 1992. It involves man and wife teams of two, racing around a gruelling course with the men carrying their wives on their backs.

What do I need to play it?

A wife, though a potential one will do.

How many friends?

Enough teams of two to make it a race.

How do I play it?

- First up you need to set out your course. The official Finnish course includes a water jump. If this isn't easy to facilitate, just ensure there's enough of a challenge to make it a decent race.

- Other suggestions might be a plank to balance on, bending poles to weave in and out of, or whatever obstacle-course paraphernalia comes to hand.

- The couples then race around the course, with the first across the finish line winning.

- The official prize in Finland is the wife's weight in beer.

Ultimate Cowpat Frisbee

What's the game?

My sister reminded me of this one recently. It was another favourite when we stayed at our aunt's house in Devon, though we hadn't come across the 'ultimate' factor as children.

You know how cowpats go all hard and crusty once they've been baked in the sun for a bit? Well, they make fantastic frisbees. Select your cowpats carefully by giving them a good prod with a stick to ensure they're dried all the way through. If you're feeling intrepid, you could add the sloppy potential of your cowpat as an additional 'lucky dip' layer to the game. You're going to have to have a good forage to find a firm enough cowpat, but if the time of year's right and the sun's done its work, you should be able to locate one that'll last you a short while at least. If it's not the height of summer, wintry frozen cowpats are a good alternative.

This is also a great way to play Frolf if you don't have a frisbee to hand (see Frolf, earlier in this chapter).

What do I need to play it?

Some dried or frozen cowpats. You'll need a good few, as depending on the particular cow's digestion they can end up rather crumbly.

How many friends?

Should be officially played with two teams of seven, with someone to act as the umpire, but you can adapt it at will to make it work in smaller groups. Oh, and avoid picking your nose until you've thoroughly washed your hands after the game.

How do I play it?

- Get into two teams, ideally with seven in each. For the purpose of clarity, the team with the cowpat frisbee is called the 'defence' and the team without is the 'offence'.

- Find a large rectangular area to play on. As guidance, a regulation field is 64 metres by 37 metres, with 'endzones' (scoring areas, similar to American football) about 20 metres deep.

- Both teams line up at the front of their endzones and the team with the cowpat throws it to one of their team members, who has moved forward into position to receive the cowpat frisbee. Players must not run with the cowpat and they're only allowed to hold it for a maximum of ten seconds. It's the player's marker's responsibility to count this out.

- Points are scored when the offence manages to penetrate the defence's endzone, and catches a pass there. Play then continues after each score.

- When a pass either fails, is intercepted or becomes a foul (for example, it's out of bounds, or contact with another player is made) the defence immediately takes possession of the cowpat and they become the offence team.

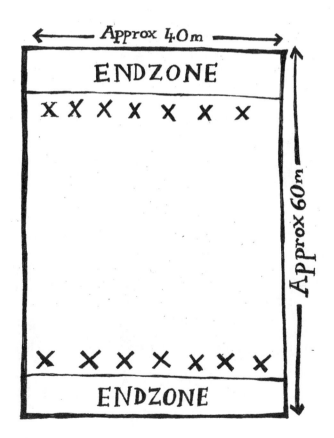

Mangold Hurling

What's the game?

A traditional Somerset game that can be traced back to the Middle Ages. During the nineteenth century its popularity peaked as it allowed the humble farm labourer a chance to compete on an equal footing with his master. Come October, the game is a highly anticipated fixture across Somerset and essentially involves lobbing a root vegetable in a field.

As mangolds are quite hard to come by these days, a turnip or swede would work just as well. But a word of caution from the Mangold Hurling Association before you play: 'Mangold Hurling is a lethal sport' and they do recommend you seek tuition before going solo (6).

What do I need to play it?

A mangold or similar sized root vegetable per player, and an extra one to act as the target. You will also need a basket to stand in.

How many friends?

At least two of you, though the more the better.

How do I play it?

- First up, you need to prepare your mangold. Chop off any unwanted foliage and ensure mud is removed to guarantee maximum aerodynamism.

- Next, you need to set up your field of play. Traditionally, the winner of the previous year's tournament ceremoniously places the basket ready for play. As it's likely to be the first time for most of you, don't worry too much about this aspect. Place your basket at an optimum casting point. Finally, you need to set out your target (a bit like in Crown Green Bowls or even Boules) – this is another mangold called the 'Norman'. This should be positioned at a reasonable distance from the pitching basket.

- Players then take it in turns to stand in the basket and on the command of 'Hurl!' players take it in turns to lob their mangolds as far as they can towards the target.

The Great Outdoors

- When all contestants have pitched their mangolds, it's the job of the 'willow' (the judge) to measure distances and decide who's the closest. Traditionally a willow branch is used as the measuring stick, which is then nicked with a cutting tool to mark out contestants' performances.

- The Mangold Hurling Association's website offers some really helpful tips on stance and style. Visit www.mangoldhurling.co.uk.

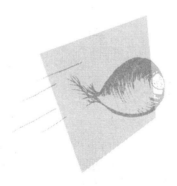

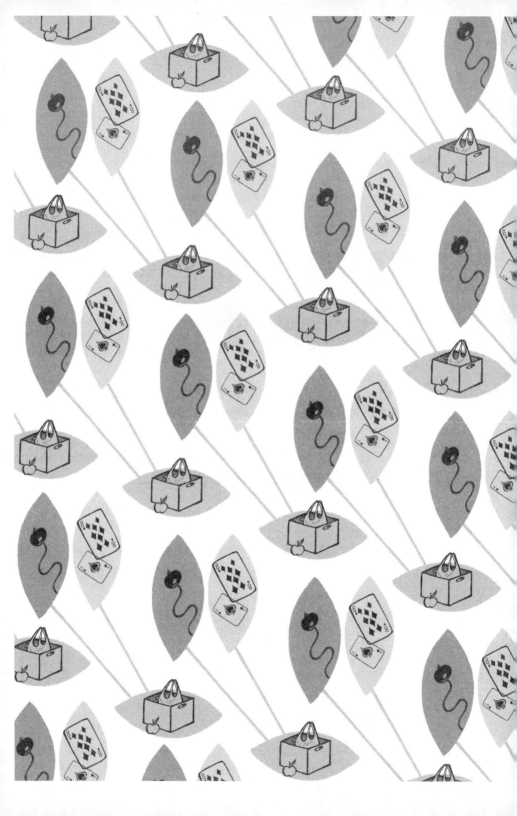

TWO

Organised Fun for Rainy Days

Most of us have a childhood memory of watching the raindrops chase down the windowpane and we can all recall the itching frustration of being cooped up inside.

I've always been a fan of extreme weather and believe there's nothing better to remind us of our place in this vast and unpredictable universe. When it rains on the Thames, we sit at the front of our houseboat watching and listening as the river's magic comes to life.

These days, British summertime seems equally likely to be drenched in rain as scorched by the sun. Whether or not this is the effect of global warming, it's a situation we have to face, particularly on holidays to the extremities of our fair isle. A bit of rain shouldn't result in a lost day of play. A rainy Saturday brings its own set of pleasures. There's nothing better to bond people over a common experience than a rain-checked British summer and a bout of indoor organised fun.

Table Rugby

What's the game?

This is one for rugby enthusiasts, or just to occupy you down the pub on a rainy afternoon. It's a great incentive to get guests to help clear up as the table needs to be empty to be able to play it. It's kept us entertained for hours on many a rainy afternoon.

What do I need to play it?

A table, a coin and two chairs.

How many friends?

At least two of you.

How do I play it?

- First up, players need to take it in turns to score a 'try'. A try is scored when a player successfully flicks a coin (using your index finger and thumb) to the other side of the table so that a part of it lays flat and hangs over the edge.
- Players get three flick attempts, and if they fail it's the next player's turn.
- If successful, they then need to flick the coin off the edge of the table using index finger and thumb, and catch it as it falls. If they manage, they score five points.
- As in the real game of rugby, to score extra points the try needs to be 'converted'.
- To convert a try the player places the coin between their index finger and thumb and then spins it before attempting to catch it mid-spin.
- Next, the player uses their two thumbs and throws the coin between the hands of another player, who has created an H with their fingers. If successful, the player scores another two points.
- First person to fifty points wins.

Human Fruit Machine

What's the game?

This one's a novel version of the noisy and now slightly archaic pub favourite. A friend of mine came across it at Bristol's St Paul's Carnival where a fun-loving father and his three sons had set up a stall. They became the hit of the weekend and earned themselves a packet as people queued up to play. It provides a brilliant afternoon's entertainment or, even better, makes a great sideshow at your local fête, festival or party.

What do I need to play it?

You'll need three bags, each containing the same set of three different fruits, along with an old-fashioned football rattle (obscure but perfect if you happen to have one). Alternatively, be creative and find or make something that sounds like the spinning of a fruit machine, such as a child's rattle. You'll also need a table and three chairs, and three cardboard boxes big enough for you to lean into (anything with about half a metre height and similar width is perfect), with their bottoms and lids cut off, leaving the four sides intact – again ideal, but not essential.

How many friends?

Four to be the fruit machine and as many as possible to bet.

How do I play it?

- Set up the table with three chairs in a row behind it. Place the cardboard boxes on the table next to each other so that when the three players sit down, they can lean into them and be shielded from what the others are doing.

- Get the three players (or the 'fruits') to sit in a line behind the table with their arms leaning into the boxes, and place their bags containing the fruit in front of them.

- The other player stands to the side of the boxes with rattle (or similar) in hand.

- Non-players are then invited to come forward and take it in turns to bet.

- As each 'punter' hands over their money, the 'rattler' shakes or spins their sound and those with the fruit reach into their bags, unseen by their colleagues, and pull out a single fruit item, holding it inside the box so it can be seen by the punter.
- The punter wins the agreed sum if the fruits simultaneously held up are all the same.

Oxford and Cambridge Boat Race

What's the game?

This is a trick in the guise of a game. I once played it on an ageing aunt and ended up with an old lady in near-apoplectic shock. It requires friends and family who can take a joke, but kids seem to love it again and again and again, yup, and again.

What do I need to play it?

A straw and a cork for each player. Something fairly shallow to make a lake out of – a roasting tray is perfect – and a table to put it on.

How many friends?

Ideally played with two to four.

How do I play it?

- Fill your lake with water and get your cork boats lined up at the start.
- The aim of the game is for players to race their boats across the lake by blowing them through a straw.
- Get the players hyped up before the start. Then, just at the point when their faces are closest to the water, the host slams the table really hard as they say, 'Go!' so all the water splashes up and soaks them.

Dudgey's Dirty Dinners

What's the game?

I think this game could be the driving force behind my friend Dudgey's splendiferous cooking talents. Thrifty Edinburgh student days meant supper was scraped from the dregs and fluff of the larder. Tinned tuna kedgeree and sausage and Branston Pickle pasta were staple features of the student house menu.

For those familiar with *Ready Steady Cook*, this follows a similar format. Two chefs, three ingredients each and some creative cookery to rustle up a supper that will delight and win the guests' votes.

What do I need to play it?

Each of the six guests must bring an ingredient with them. A selection of basic culinary essentials should also be available – salt, pepper, oil, garlic and so on.

How many friends?

Ideally eight. Two chefs, and six people who each bring an ingredient and also have the pleasure/displeasure of judging the food.

How do I play it?

- Guests arrive bearing one cooking ingredient each. They should be told to bring either a protein- or carbohydrate-based item, and then a random 'curve ball' ingredient of their choice.
- The chefs are then challenged to cook a dish each in an agreed time period using the collected supplies. Distribute the food among each of the competing chefs, ensuring that each chef has something from each food group described above. Chefs are then told which course they're cooking.
- The chefs are judged and awarded points for taste, creativity and skill.

Conkers

What's the game?

Conkers has been a playground favourite for centuries and continues to be the autumn game of choice for schoolchildren across the UK. A 2008 poll in the *Daily Telegraph* of 2,000 schoolchildren named it as their number one favourite (7).

Although a British invention, the game has since gone international. From Canada to France, wherever the horse chestnut prospers, schoolchildren can be found hanging the shiny blighters on string and smashing their mates' ones to pieces. Its popularity has grown to such an extent that a world championship is held each year in Northamptonshire. The French, who make themselves a regular feature at the event, claim to have a strong strategy behind their game. In a recent *Times* quote the French Federation's chairman Stephane Jally stated, 'Conkers is like rugby. The British invented it, but we do it better.' (8)

There's a pub along the river from where we live that always has conker accoutrements on the bar come the fresh winds of autumn. We spend most Saturdays in September chugging down the river to plonk ourselves on our favourite bar stools and challenge the locals to a game.

Although tempting to come up with a variation, some classics shouldn't be messed with.

What do I need to play it?

Conkers, string and scissors.

How many friends?

A minimum of two, though a tournament is a great way to spend an autumn Saturday down the pub.

How do I play it?

- First up, select your conker on the basis of form, symmetry and lack of cracks.
- Next, prepare for battle. Drill a hole down the middle using a sharp skewer (or even a power drill if you're getting serious) and thread a piece of string through the hole. You need one that's about 25 centimetres in

length. If the hole is drilled badly you can weaken the strength of the conker. Try to drill or skewer as straight as possible. Avoid the lighter-coloured circle on top as it's not as waxy as the rest of the skin and therefore more likely to crack.

- Once you've threaded your string through, tie multiple knots at the bottom to ensure it doesn't fall off. One tip from Simon at the pub is to also tie a knot at the point the string comes out of the top of the conker. This prevents it sliding up the string and maximises its force when in play.
- Once conkers are threaded and contestants are ready to play, two players face each other with their conkers hanging down on the string and the string wrapped around their hands a couple of times for extra support.
- Players then take it in turns to thwack and hopefully crack their opponent's conker, by stretching the string taught with the hitting conker drawn towards them, and then using this length to target the full force towards the opponent's hanging conker on its release.
- If a player misses, they are allowed two extra goes.
- If the strings tangle, the first player to call 'Strings!' gets an extra shot.
- If a player strikes and causes their opponent's conker to spin in a full circle, the player gets another go.
- If a player drops their conker or it's knocked out of their hand, the other player can shout 'Stamps!' and then is able to jump on it, aiming to crack it. If the first player cries 'No stamps!' first, then the other player is not allowed to stamp on it.
- The winner is the one whose conker lasts the longest. Each time a conker defeats another it clocks up its victim's numbers. In a contest of two new conkers the winner's conker thus becomes 'a oner' (bring back memories?). If the same conker beats another successful conker who was, say, 'a fourer', the winning conker then goes on to take on its defeated conker's score – making it 'a fiver'.
- Now, when I was younger there was a whole lot of jiggery-pokery around how to make your conkers as un-crackable as possible, from soaking them in vinegar to baking them in the oven. I'm not sure how effective any of these are. I remember being convinced that doing both was the secret behind my 'elevener' at school. One tip I recently heard which does make a lot of sense is: if you put a selection of conkers in water and some of them float, discard these ones and use the heavier and denser ones at the bottom of the bowl as they're likely to be stronger.

Are You There, Moriarty?

What's the game?

This is a Victorian parlour game where two players take part in a duel. You need to make sure you have enough space to play it. A few friends and I caused some rather nasty damage when we last played, so do be careful.

What do I need to play it?

Two blindfolds and two rolled-up newspapers.

How many friends?

Two to play, and as many as are around to watch and wait their turn.

How do I play it?

- Get everyone to sit around. Blindfold the duelling pair and get them to lie on their backs, head-to-head, with about a metre of space between them. A good way to measure if there's enough of a gap is to get them to shake hands as a mark of respect for their opponent before duelling begins.
- The starting player then shouts 'Are you there, Moriarty?' and the opponent responds 'Yes'. At this signal, the players then attempt to bash their opponent with their rolled-up newspaper while maintaining the same flat position on the ground, without moving their legs or backs.
- The first player to be hit is out and the next player steps in to take their place.

Household Horseshoes

What's the game?

The traditional horseshoe game found at country fairs across the country can also be turned into an indoor event when played with a toilet brush and holder. Great for inactive game playing while nestled on the sofa, and ideal to see whose turn it is to make the tea.

What do I need to play it?

A toilet brush in its holder and anything shaped in a ring, such as a piece of rope tied in a circle, a bracelet or pastry cutter. You need three for each player, though if you're short you can pass them between you.

How many friends?

A minimum of two players with no more than four. It loses its appeal if there's too much waiting around.

How do I play it?

- Maintain a comfortable position on the sofa and position the toilet brush at an achievable, though challenging, distance.
- Players take it in turns to score points by getting their 'ring thing' over the stick at the top of the toilet brush holder.

The Nail Game

What's the game?

This is an Alpine classic, known to anyone who's been on an Austrian skiing holiday that included a visit to the local tavern. It's a competition of judgement and strength where players compete to be the one to hammer the nail all the way into the log. It provides a great opportunity for male bonding as it combines strength, hammer dexterity and a dose of competition in one neat 'hanging out at the bar' package.

What do I need to play it?

A log, a hammer and some four-to-six-inch nails.

How many friends?

I wouldn't recommend playing it with more than eight of you as it could mean too much waiting around.

How do I play it?

- The object of the game is to be the person who takes the final strike to get the nail into the log.
- First, tap a good-sized nail into a solid log or wooden block.
- Each player takes the hammer and strikes the nail in turn. If they are particularly bold they might go for getting the nail all the way in. I've never seen this happen, though am sure that if you're a challenger for the Austrian Championship it's a possibility.
- If, as usually is the case, the player only gets it a short way in, the hammer is handed around the group, with the last striker getting the point.

Dress-Up Sunday

What's the game?

This is less of a game and more of a way to entertain yourself and a group of friends. It's completely purposeless other than to show off your creative skills in putting a fancy-dress outfit together.

What do I need to play it?

Some creative flair or some cash to spend at the fancy-dress shop.

How many friends?

You'd look a bit silly on your own, so I'd suggest at least two of you, though a big group makes it much more fun.

How do I play it?

- Choose the theme.
- Ask your friends to meet you at the restaurant of your choice all trussed up in your fancy-dress creations.
- If you don't like them, don't turn up. That was a joke. That would be very cruel.

The Advert Game

What's the game?

This is a game to play when you're stuck indoors in front of the television. A bit like in the TV show *The Royle Family* where they have to guess the value of every item on *Antiques Roadshow*, it makes TV watching more entertaining when the viewing content gets a bit dull. You do need to be tuned into a commercial channel to play.

What do I need to play it?

A TV tuned into a channel that has commercials.

How many friends?

As many as are around and watching TV.

How do I play it?

- Tune in, sit back and wait for the commercial break.
- First one to guess what the advert is from the opening bars of the music scores a point.

Pants Roulette

What's the game?

This game came out of travels around South-East Asia. As the monsoon rains poured down outside, my travelling partner and I lay in our stark room staring up at our ceiling fan. This one only really works if you've got a ceiling fan, so bear it in mind for summer holidays in balmy destinations. NB: Different scanties have different velocities when chucked in the air.

What do I need to play it?

A ceiling fan and some pants or female scanties.

How many friends?

As many as are in the room.

How do I play it?

- Put one pair of pants on a circular ceiling fan while it's turned off.
- Players place bets on which wall the pants are going to fly off and hit.
- Turn the fan on, slowly building up to full speed until the pants propel themselves off and splat against the wall.
- Correct guess wins the dosh.

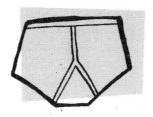

Look of the Season

What's the game?

This one's great for aspiring fashion designers or anyone with a bit of creative flair. It was born out of a birthday weekend in a thatched cottage in the countryside. It culminated in a fully commentated fashion show, with us all wearing the winner's new designs for the rest of the evening.

What do I need to play it?

Whatever you can lay your hands on – bin bags, kitchen roll, curtains, sheets, feather duster – you get the idea.

How many friends?

As many teams as you like. Would suggest no more than four players in each team.

How do I play it?

- Players get into teams and are given a set amount of time to go away and design their outfit from whatever they can lay their hands on.
- The only rule is that actual clothing is banned. Outfits need to be customised from whatever can be found around the house – bin bags, kitchen roll, kitchen utensils, bath mats, and so on. You can choose to have one model with the rest of the group creating, or you might opt to have the full team wearing a series of the designed clothes.
- Points should be awarded for creativity and inspired accessorising.

Card Games

Who would have thought that a pack of fifty-two different pieces of card could deliver such enduring and global entertainment value? The game of cards has to be the most well-travelled piece of organised fun this planet has seen.

It's believed that card playing originated in China in around the tenth century, when intrepid travelling Chinamen improvised their domino game by creating domino pieces out of bits of card. From here playing cards were born. They formally emerged as elaborately engraved woodcuts, which aided their passage to Europe as a sellable commodity and made them the game of choice for the Euro 'it' crowd. It was those aesthetically refined French folk who were behind the development of the four suits – diamonds, hearts, spades and clubs – and they were also responsible for simplifying the shapes and introducing the use of flat colour, clearing the path to mass production. By the fourteenth century when the art of printing was mastered, cards and the choice of games to play was opened to the masses.

Everybody needs a couple of card games in their repertoire. It's a civilised and somehow bonding way to fill a rainy afternoon. The following three have been selected based on their simplicity and family appeal, and they should keep you entertained and distracted from the rain for a good few hours.

Pig

What's the game?

Pig is great fun to play with adults and kids and will easily while away a rainy afternoon. It's a card game that works well in big groups as well as small and, for those whingeing of addled brains, it's very easy to pick up.

What do I need to play it?

A pack of cards.

How many friends?

Works well in small groups of four, but lots of fun for larger groups of up to 13.

How do I play it?

- First of all, you need to get yourself set up by counting out four of the same number or face card for each player. It doesn't matter which ones you choose as the different cards have no intrinsic value.

- Once sorted, discard the remainder of the deck, shuffle the pack and deal them out so that everyone has four cards each.

- The aim of the game is to be the first to collect a matching set of four to win the round.

- To start, players simultaneously choose their least favourite card and place it face down to their left-hand side for their neighbour to pick up as the dealer says 'Go!' Players then pick up the card the person to their right has laid down. If it matches anything in their hand then they should probably keep it; if not, it might be one they choose to discard on the next turn.

- The dealer then says 'Go!' again and players continue choosing and rejecting a card before picking the one up that's placed to their right. Play continues until someone gets four matching cards, and they put their finger on the tip of their nose. On seeing this all players must copy the action, and whoever's last earns a P.

- The first player to earn the letters P-I-G is out and one of the sets of four cards is removed from play before the game plays on. Play continues in the same way until the last player is left in and is declared the winner.

- NB: You can make the game last longer by dealing eight cards to each player, so that the aim is for each person to collect two sets of four cards.

Cheat

What's the game?

Cheat is one of the many enduring games that has travelled the world and stayed intact. It can be rolled out on a beach in Goa with a motley crew of hippy travellers or on a Saga holiday cruise, and you can be pretty certain of the same positive 'Oh yes, I know that game' response. If you don't know it, then it's definitely one to store in your memory banks. The objective of the game is to try to convince fellow players that you're not lying. Poker faces at the ready.

What do I need to play it?

A pack of cards.

How many friends?

Works with groups of any size between three and ten.

How do I play it?

- The aim of the game is to be the first to get rid of all your cards.
- First of all, deal out the entire pack of cards to the gathered players.
- To play the game, each player takes it in turn to lay a card or cards facing down one on top of the other, and say which card they've put down. You can lay anything, from just one to all four cards of a particular number or face card, for example one, two or three jacks. Subsequent players follow the same rules, but their cards must be from the same number or one higher or lower than the previous player has laid, so, for example, if the first player lays two aces, the second player can lay aces, kings or twos.
- This is what you are *supposed* to do, but the players may not in fact be laying the cards they claim to be laying!
- Each time a card or cards are laid down, the player has to state what the card is, i.e. 'A two,' or 'Three jacks.' If any of the other players think or in fact know that the other player is cheating (particularly if they've got the card that player is claiming to have just laid down) then they should shout 'Cheat!'

- If the challenge is correct, the cheating player has to pick up the stack of cards in the middle. If wrong, then the player who shouted the incorrect accusation has to pick them up.
- After the challenge is resolved, play continues in the same order, with the next player laying down whichever card they choose.
- The fun bit starts as players need to get rid of cards they're stuck with and the cheating starts to get more prolific. Keep an eye out for people stuffing rogue cards in flowerpots or down their trousers, leaving a cheater's trail when they nip off to the toilet.

Trumps

What's the game?

Trumps, or Knockout as it is also known, was a family favourite in our household when I was a nipper. I can remember huddling by the fire for hours listening intently as our dad taught us the art of the game. Before long, we were hooked, and became obsessed with playing at any opportunity. Under bedcovers at midnight or at the crack of dawn before school, we could be found shuffling and dealing like pros with the twinkle of a hustler in our eyes. Thankfully, as with any new toy, the interest soon wore off and no subsequent gambling addictions emerged.

The aim of the game is to win as many of the seven rounds as possible, by winning 'tricks' in each round.

What do I need to play it?

A pack of cards.

How many friends?

The maximum number of players is seven, but it works best in groups of four to five.

How do I play it?

- To get started, the dealer shuffles the pack and deals out seven cards to each of the players. The aim of the game is to win the most tricks. To win a trick you must lay down the highest card number or the highest 'trump' (the chosen suit that is worth more than any of the others in that round).

- To decide which suit is trumps, the top card from the un-dealt pack is turned upwards, and the card shown indicates which suit it will be.

- The player to the left of the dealer leads by placing a card face upwards, with the other players doing the same thing in a clockwise direction. Players must follow suit if they have a card from the suit that was first laid; if they can't, they should play a trump; if they have no trumps then any card can be used. Once everyone has laid a card, the highest card of the suit that was laid first wins that trick. However, if someone played a trump then the highest trump wins.

- Each player then lays another card, and the game plays on.
- Once the first round is completed, the winner of the most tricks wins that round. The dealer then deals out six cards to each player and the game continues in the same fashion. In each round one less card is dealt to each player, until the remaining players have just one card each, with the winner of the previous round nominating which suit will be trumps.
- If a player doesn't win any tricks in any given round then they're out of play.
- If a round is drawn, the deck is cut and those drawing pick a card. The highest, irrespective of suit, wins the right to nominate trumps.
- The winner is the last person left in.

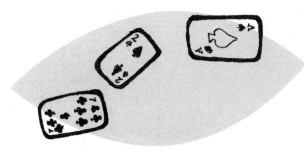

Rainy Days

THREE

Organised Fun for the Beach or Campsite

Perhaps it's the exploding popularity of festivals that's made camping cool again. All those urbanites who'd previously never had a brush with canvas can now be found discussing the varying merits of gas-fired stoves and pop-up tents. Although this might lead to camping traditionalists grumbling about packed sites, this burgeoning following can certainly be thanked for their growing variety.

I love how wholesome camping makes me feel; I get a feel-good booster just at the thought of getting back to basics. There's something pleasingly feral about mud-marinated chicken, and flossing with blades of grass as you laze around the campfire of an evening.

We're fairly rigid in our camping habits. We go to the same campsite on the same week every year – a beautiful spot where the rugged Welsh hills meet the sea and the summer heather casts a purple haze across the bay – and this chapter contains the games we've played to fill many a gold-drenched summer afternoon in this beautiful setting. You'll find all sorts of games for playing on the beach or in a field, and there are also a few suggestions for those days when you're stuck inside your rain-lashed tent.

Tide Race

What's the game?

The challenge is to see who can stay on their desert island the longest. Islands are created on a flat sandy beach as the tide is coming in by shovelling and packing sand into piles large enough for you and your teammates to stand on. The winner of the game is the team who manages to stay on their desert island the longest.

What do I need to play it?

Something to dig with (a piece of driftwood or your hands would work), and a sandy beach with an incoming tide.

How many friends?

At least two, or as many as you like. All must be strong swimmers and happy to get wet.

How do I play it?

- Get into teams of however many you want. Sizes can vary depending on how well you rate your chances of staying on your desert island, based on the volume of people and manpower for building versus the lightness of a single player.
- Each team builds their island, close to the tide on a big flat sandy beach with shallow water.
- Once completed, all stand on your mound. The team that stays driest on their mound the longest wins.

Flotsam and Jetsam Boules

What's the game?

There's a house we often stay at in Cornwall that's decorated with flotsam and jetsam beach finds. Sculptural driftwood adorns the mantelpiece and colourful bottle lids are framed to create a Hirst-like painting that hangs above the fireplace. There's an old fishing net woven with dried seaweed and old rope that hangs in the hallway like a medieval seaside tapestry.

It's a tradition on these Cornish holidays to hold a Boules tournament down on the beach. One year, an unnamed friend forgot to bring the boules set, so we had to improvise with what we could find. The house is also adorned with colourful pendant-like boat buoys and we decided to collect these together and take them down to the beach for a game. We used a pebble for the jack and sticks to mark out the playing area. The novel equipment gave a whole new angle to the event and started an annual tradition of playing with whatever we find on the beach.

NB: If you're on a particularly neat beach and can't find anything to hand, your flip-flops, sandals or even pebbles work just as well.

What do I need to play it?

Flotsam and jetsam finds, or a pair of flip-flops per player.

How many friends?

A minimum of two players.

How do I play it?

- Mark out your boules court. If on a beach, simply draw it out in the sand, or lay out sticks to mark the parameters.
- Whoever's playing first throws the jack out into the designated playing area.
- Players then take it in turns to chuck their boule replacement and try to get it as close to the jack as possible without stepping over the marked throwing line.
- Players then continue to take it in turns to get as close to the jack as possible while also trying to knock their opponents' boules out of the way.

The Beach or Campsite

- When everyone has thrown, the winner of the round is the person closest to the jack, and the winner must calculate their score by giving themselves one point for each of their boules nearest the jack and ahead of the next closest player's best boule.
- The winning player is then the one to throw the jack to start the next round, and the first player to score 13 wins the game.

Beach Volcano

What's the game?

This is less of a game and more of a challenge. It's a great one to play with kids, or to fill a long lazy afternoon on the sands. A competitive element could of course be built in – you could aim for the longest smoking volcano, or the last volcano standing when the tide comes.

What do I need to play it?

Sand, sculpting hands, some kindling and a lighter.

How many friends?

As few or as many as you like.

How do I play it?

- Make a pile of sand, tunnel a hole in the middle down to the ground and then tunnel in from the side until your two passages meet.
- Get creative with your design – seaweed, grass and bushes, colourful eruptions, and so on.
- Then push some paper or driftwood into the bottom of your passage and light a fire. Smoke should soon billow from the top like an exploding volcano. To complete the apocalypse, you should time it so the tide comes in once the spectacular has had some time to show off. This will make sure the volcano is fully extinguished before you leave the beach.

Sand Skittles

What's the game?

One of the oldest games in the world, the fun value of Skittles has ensured its durability, with many references made to the sport throughout history.

This is a classic English pub game of Skittles played on the beach with recycled plastic water bottles filled with sand.

What do I need to play it?

Nine plastic water bottles filled with sand and with their lids screwed back on, and something round and heavy to be the ball. We've used a swede in the past but they can be hard to come by if you're playing in summer. A round pebble is a great alternative. Ideally you'll need a few balls to save you running around.

How many friends?

A minimum of two players.

How do I play it?

- First up, prepare your kit. Fill your nine bottles with equal amounts of sand and screw the lids back on. If you're using a swede, give it a bit of a trim to make it as round as possible.

- Set your nine skittles up so they form an equilateral triangle.

- Players then have two turns to roll to see how many sand bottles they can knock down. If your ball object is lacking in roundness, you might have to adopt a throw opposed to a roll.

- The easiest way to score is by adding a point for every sand bottle that's knocked over.

Brave the Wave

What's the game?

Richard, a friend who grew up on the beaches of Norfolk, used to play this as a teenager on the way home from school. It's really a game of daring, hence its popularity among teenage boys. Players compete to be the last one to run from the wave as it crashes on the shoreline.

I recently heard of an urban equivalent called Splash and Dash. Nothing to do with inconsiderate toilet visitors, it instead follows the same rules outlined below but involves large puddles and passing cars.

What do I need to play it?

A beach with big crashing waves. Children should make sure an adult is watching them.

How many friends?

You can play it by yourself if you like, but you might look a bit silly running in and then away from the waves on your own fully clothed.

How do I play it?

- All line up and face the shoreline on a beach with crashing waves.
- The last person to run away is the winner.
- The alternative is to play it as a knockout. The first person to run away from the waves is out, which does mean a fair share of soaking, but that's all part of the fun.

- The obvious note of safety is required here. Only play on a beach you know well, make sure there's an easy getaway and be absolutely sure there isn't a big rip in the water.

Skimming

What's the game?

Stone Skimming has always evoked images of father and son silhouetted against the sunset as they skim their stones from the beach. Its nostalgic appeal ensures it's passed on down the line, guaranteeing it a long and healthy future.

My dad taught us the art of skimming while on a family holiday on Islay, a small island in the Scottish Outer Hebrides. It used to infuriate us girls that the boys seemed to have an innate ability to master the flick and be able to judge the impetus required to bounce a smooth flat pebble across the water. Stone Skimming is an art that is attained through practice.

What do I need to play it?

A collection of small, flat pebbles, and a stretch of water.

How many friends?

Perfect to play solo or with however many you like.

How do I play it?

- Carefully select a collection of small, flat pebbles. Everyone has a different view on which works best, but I've always found the rounder and flatter the better.
- Stand on the shore or bank and use a flicking motion with your hand so

that your pebble bounces across the water.
- The winner is the person whose pebble achieves the most bounces as it flies across the water.
- An alternative version is to bounce them across a river so they land (ideally) in the same spot on the other side. We often play this off our houseboat, and have just about mastered the degree of flick required to land the stone so that it hits the bench on the opposite bank, obviously when it's free of dozing grannies.

Sleeping-Bag Sumo

What's the game?

This is a great camping game. We played it on a Welsh hillside at a farm where a group of us have camped for years. The added element of playing on a slope is that when you're knocked down, you end up rolling down the hill, as it's a nightmare to get up. A word of warning: the smell of cowpats is almost impossible to remove. Choose a sheep-grazed field if you can.

What do I need to play it?

Sleeping bags and pillows.

How many friends?

At least two of you, but as many as you want.

How do I play it?

- Everyone stands in their sleeping bag and grabs their pillow.
- The object of the game is to knock everyone down. Once down, you're out. Last man standing is the winner.
- Get in your sleeping bag with your feet at the closed end. Grab your pillow and start bashing!

Beach Sculpture Competition

What's the game?

Sand sculpting is an art played out on beaches around the world. Even the sandy banks of the Thames regularly play host to such artists.

A friend came across a Beach Sculpture Competition on a Dorset beach where the most fantastically imaginative objects where being created. A young Hugh Fearnley-Whittingstall, soon to become the celebrity chef, was an enthusiastic participant. Rather than spending hours crafting his idea, he went off to do a spot of fishing. Fifteen minutes before the judging took place he arrived back on the beach with a net full of mackerel. He proceeded to sculpt a voluptuous mermaid's tail over his legs, below his bare torso, and then got his mackerel-filled basket and decorated the tail with a glistening fishy finish. His inspired approach won him the competition and he celebrated by barbecuing his catch and sharing it with his fellow contestants.

What do I need to play it?

Whatever flotsam and jetsam you can find to fuel your ideas.

How many friends?

You could easily play it by yourself, but a few friends (as few or as many as you like) make it a lot more fun.

How do I play it?

- Players are given a set amount of time to create their masterpieces. Part of that needs to be spent scouring for materials.
- At the end of this time, players are judged and prizes awarded.

Washing-Up Bowl Grand National

What's the game?

Racing down the hill with your bum stuck in a washing-up bowl and your legs in the air is a novel way to pass an afternoon. This is another great one for the campsite, as everyone has their washing-up bowl with them. As the traditional washing-up bowl does require a small bottom to fit in, you can be creative to identify alternative mounts, such as tea trays, or plastic storage crates. If you're playing on sand dunes, sadly washing-up bowls tend to end up sinking into the sand. A boogie board or anything with a large flat surface is the preferred sand dune mount.

What do I need to play it?

Ideally a washing-up bowl but a tray would do. I've even attempted it on a bin bag.

How many friends?

You need more than one of you to make it a race.

How do I play it?

- Get to the top of the hill or sand dune with your washing-up bowl, or designated mount.
- On the signal, all hurtle yourselves down the hill.
- A note as always on safety. Wisest to avoid grassy slopes with cliffs at the end and make sure you practise the use of your feet as a brake. The technique is to stick them forwards, enabling you to dig your heels in if needed.

Human Whirligig

What's the game?

Invented in around 4000 BC by the ancient Egyptians, this game involves spinning your friends to create a human whirligig. It lacks a competitive element but will leave you falling in a giddy, giggly mass. Scholars named it the Star Game.

What do I need to play it?

Just yourselves and somewhere soft to land; a sandy beach is ideal.

How many friends?

Two strong boys or girls to do the spinning, and four lighter people to be spun.

How do I play it?

- Get yourself into two trios and decide on which two of you are going to be the 'spinners', and which two the ones to be spun.
- The spinners then stand back-to-back while the other four players stand about 30 centimetres in front of each of the spinners' arms.
- Players then take each other's hands, and those to be spun lean back to take up the full slack of their arms
- Decide which way the spinners will spin and then on the word 'Go!' they spin their partners, who run in small tight circles while continuing to lean out. Meanwhile the spinners maintain their back-to-back position as they move.
- Last trio standing wins.
- NB: This can also be played with four players instead of six, with each spinner holding both hands of the person they are spinning.

The Beach or Campsite

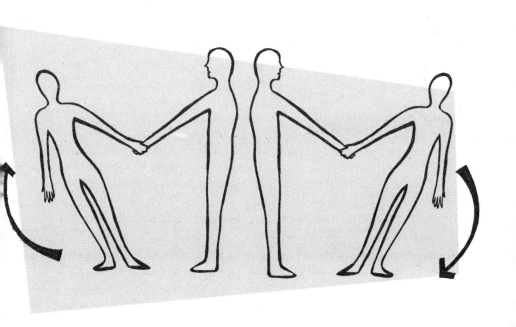

Kebab Skewer Darts

What's the game?

This game formed part of our annual Organised Fun Olympics that this year took place in Cornwall. Nick was this year's winner, and Kebab Skewer Darts was the game that won the tournament for him.

What do I need to play it?

A sandy beach and some kebab skewers.

How many friends?

Works best in small groups of two to eight.

How do I play it?

- First of all, you need to draw out a giant dartboard in the sand. Choose a flat area, with wet, firm sand being best to enable the dart to stand up. To keep it simple I'd suggest drawing three rings, each carrying a certain number of points.
- Next, draw a line in the sand at a predetermined distance from the dartboard.
- Players then have three goes to score as many points as they can by firing their skewers using the same action as in a game of darts. The obvious warning needs to be added to make sure you play with caution and ensure there are no young children close by.
- Depending on how good you get, you need to decide whether a skewer that doesn't stand up in the sand when thrown counts as a point.

Welly Wanging

What's the game?

This was another key feature of our recent Organised Fun Olympics. It's exactly like a Hammer Throw event, but with wellies instead. I'd recommend adopting the underarm 'wang' as quite often the unequal weighting of a traditional welly causes the overarm lob to pitch unpredictably. Wang with the sole facing forwards, as air getting caught in the welly as it flies through the sky slows it down and impacts on final measured distance. I've thought about this a little too much, haven't I?

What do I need to play it?

A welly for each player and something (sticks, coats, and so on) to identify individual player lobs.

How many friends?

More than just yourself to make it fun.

How do I play it?

- Set a wanging line.
- Stand behind the line and launch your welly.
- The umpire then needs to replace the landed welly with the player's marker.
- Each player gets three wangs and the longest is taken as the winner's distance.
- The winner is the one who throws their welly the farthest.

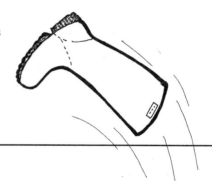

Beach Rounders

What's the game?

Rounders was my favourite game at school. I can still picture the knobbly knees and hard-as-nails stares that stepped down from the opposing school's bus. As most played it at school, it should be fairly easy for people to remember. It's a perfect game to play on a wide-open sandy beach with a group of family or friends.

The game originated in Ireland, though it's thought to be an adaptation of English Baseball, which can be found dating back to Tudor times. It is generally accepted that the game of Baseball popular across the US today is in fact derived from the Irish game of Rounders.

For those not familiar with the game, it's a cross between Cricket and Baseball, where teams alternate at batting and points are scored by racing around a circuit without getting caught or stumped out.

What do I need to play it?

A bat and a ball, though a thick stick and a tennis ball would be more than adequate, and some clothes or stones to mark out the points in the field.

How many friends?

Each team should ideally have nine players, with one person acting as umpire.

How do I play it?

- First of all, get into your two teams and agree what position everyone's going to play. The fielding team should assume their positions, with the batting team lining up behind the batsman's square, ready to take their turn.

- The aim of the game is to hit a ball far enough that the batter has the chance to race around the four posts without getting stumped or caught out.

- 'No ball' is called if the ball is bowled above the head or below the knee, if it bounces on the way to the batter or if it's bowled straight at the body. If you run on a 'no ball', you can only go to first base and no more than three 'no balls' are allowed to be called.

- If the batter hits the ball behind them they can only run to first base.
- If a good ball is bowled, the batter must hit it as far as they can and then race around the four bases to touch in at fourth base to score a rounder. If they cannot make it all the way around without getting out, they can stop at any base along the way.
- Other scoring is as follows:
  - Half a rounder if fourth post is reached but the ball hasn't been hit.
  - Half a rounder if second post is reached when the ball was hit (optional rule).
  - Half a rounder for an obstruction by a fielder.
  - Half a rounder for two consecutive no balls (same batter).
- Players are out if the ball is caught by the opposite team straight off the bat, or if a fielder catches the ball while their foot is on their base before the batter has reached it. If there are two players on one base one of you is out, and a player can also cause someone on their team to be out if they continue to run towards the next base, meaning the player on the base they're running to has to run on. This player becomes out if the ball returns to the bowler's hands and the running player is still between bases.
- The team with the most rounders wins.

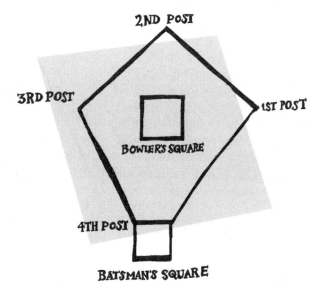

2ND POST

3RD POST

1ST POST

BOWLER'S SQUARE

4TH POST

BATSMAN'S SQUARE

French Cricket

What's the game?

French Cricket has nothing to do with the French, but is a milder adaptation of its namesake sport. It's generally believed that the name is designed to mock the French by naming a lesser style of the English classic sport after them. More importantly, it requires little kit to play and is perfect for beach or campsite.

What do I need to play it?

A tennis ball and a bat of sorts. You can fashion yourself one from whatever you have to hand. We once used one of those barbecue grills with a handle. It worked perfectly.

How many friends?

One batter and any number of fieldsmen.

How do I play it?

- The objective of the game is to prevent your legs being hit by the ball, using the bat to protect them.
- The bowler bowls underarm, aiming at the batter's legs. The batter holds the bat in front of their legs and is not allowed to move them when the ball is bowled towards them.
- If the batsman misses the ball, they're not allowed to move. They then have to try to hit the next ball facing the same way as before, which can result in some funny angles being used and you can get yourself into an awful pickle trying to bat a ball backwards.
- The ball is bowled from where it ended up after its previous delivery.

- If the batsman hits the ball they are allowed to move their feet to face the new direction the ball will be bowled from. To score a run the player must pass the bat all the way around their body, but should stop as soon as the ball is returned to the bowler. A player stays in until they are caught or got out, or is out if the ball hits them below the knee. It's then the fielder or bowler's turn to bat, whichever one got the previous player out. Any number of fielders can stand around the batsman and any fielder is able to hit the batsman's legs with the ball.
- The player who scores the most runs is the winner.

Sand-Burying Competition

What's the game?

First team to bury their teammate in the sand up to their neck, wins.

Hula-Hoop Relay

What's the game?

They say games are a good form of therapy, and that doesn't only apply to the playing part. This confession of one of my most humiliating experiences is one way of letting go of inhibitions. My mediocre running skills got me selected to represent my school in the first leg of a relay race at an inter-school sports day. I can clearly remember chatting to people in the stand as I stood waiting for the off. I was soon aware of a loud roar of laughter and looked up to realise I'd missed the start of the race, and ruined it for my team and school. To add insult to injury the stadium crowd behind me were falling about in stitches at my foolishness. The moral of the tale: clean your ears.

The next game is an adaptation of the classic relay race but with the improvisation of a Hula Hoop being passed down the line. The art of playing with a hoop has engaged children for centuries. The whipping hoop was a cane hoop that children used to chase down the street with a stick. The 1950s saw a reinvention of the classic by Wham-O-Toys, and in 1957 the world witnessed the birth of the Hula Hoop.

What do I need to play it?

A Hula Hoop for each team.

How many friends?

Enough for two teams to make it a race.

How do I play it?

- Get into two teams and spread out parallel to each other in two lines.
- The person at the top of the line starts by completing three successful spins of the hoop round your waist, and passing it down the line for the next person to do the same, and so on.
- First team to finish wins.

The Beach or Campsite

The Falling Down Game

What's the game?

The Falling Down Game was our preferred beach entertainment when I lived in Australia. It was rolled out at each and every beach lounging opportunity and had the Aussies looking on in bemusement as us daft Pommies hurled ourselves to the ground. Make sure you're playing on soft sand or else you might end up with some nasty bruises.

What do I need to play it?

Some soft sand to land on, and a digital camera.

How many friends?

At least two to compete, and one to be the judge.

How do I play it?

- It's nothing more complicated than being the first to throw yourself to the floor. Players must ensure their upper torso hits the sand first – knees don't count!
- We always use a digital camera as more often than not it's a close call to identify the winner.

Tent Shadows

What's the game?

This one will take you back to Enid Blyton camping days.

What do I need to play it?

A tent and a torch, and you'll need to wait until it's dark to play.

How many friends?

Great played on your own, though a friend makes it more fun.

How do I play it?

- Wait until it's dark outside. Take it in turns to create shapes with your hands and project these onto the tent walls using torchlight.
- Points can be awarded for creativity and how easy they are to identify.
- Adults can also play the Kama Sutra version, which I'm sure needs little explanation.

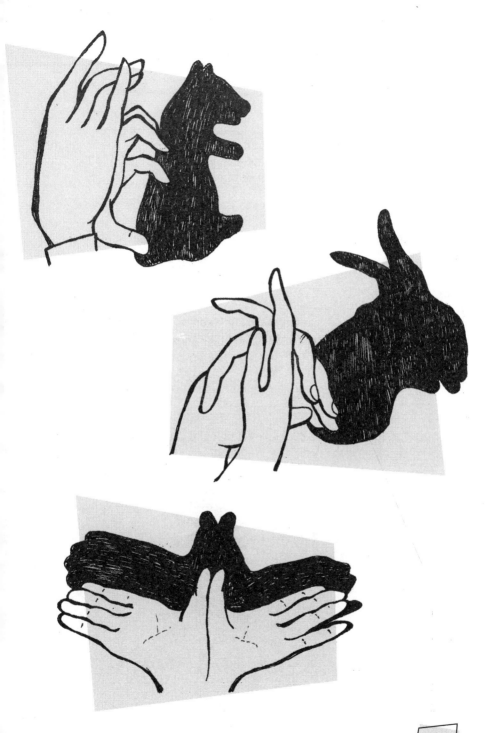

The Radio Game

What's the game?

This one's a brilliant way to fill a rain-sodden afternoon in a tent. You do need one of those portable radios, but they are ever so cheap to pick up from a petrol station, supermarket or jumble sale.

What do I need to play it?

A radio, and a knowledge of song lyrics gives a strong advantage.

How many friends?

You'd sound a bit silly playing it on your own, particularly given the lack of sound insulation in a tent.

How do I play it?

- Tune into a preferred radio station, ideally one that plays a musical genre that you're familiar with. There are loads out there that constantly play all the classics.
- Wait until a song starts to play, then after four seconds of the introduction bars, turn the sound down and whoever's turn it is has to carry on singing the song.
- After about five seconds (though this can be shortened and lengthened depending on how good you get) turn the sound back up again.
- Points are awarded for how well you've managed to keep to the song tempo and sing the right words at the right time. You can also award additional points for lyric knowledge and singing prowess or awfulness.

The Beach or Campsite

Human Crufts

What's the game?

Human Crufts is one of the many brilliant games invented by the wonderful Bestival Festival team at Camp Bestival. The event involves pairs of friends (one of whom pretends to be the pooch and the other the owner) competing in an agility class, a freestyle performance and a beauty contest.

What do I need to play it?

Some obstacles for the agility course and a range of fancy dress items for the beauty contest. You also need to make some large score cards so that each judge has a sheet of paper with a single number on it from 1 to 10. A dog lead per competing pair is also a useful accessory.

How many friends?

This one works best in big groups.

How do I play it?

- Decide on your judging panel (ideally three people) and get everyone else to pair up and decide who's the pooch and who's the owner.
- Pairs then go away and practise their show routine (a freestyle performance of their choosing) and the agility class, and agree on the outfit for their beauty contest.
- Meanwhile the judges set up the obstacle course – think along the lines of planks to balance on, obstacles to jump over and, if you can get your hands on one, a tube to tunnel through.
- Contestants then compete in the three classes and are scored out of ten by the judges, who hold up a score card at the end of each performance.
- The competing pair with the highest score at the end of the competition wins.

FOUR

After-Dinner Organised Fun: Short Games

After dinner offers a golden time for organised fun for all the family – and not just at Christmas. It's when stuffed guests sit back on their haunches and allow their guzzling to settle; it's when conversation lulls and everyone starts to relax and feel slightly silly; in all, it's the perfect moment to introduce a focus to the evening's proceedings, encourage people to break out of their comfort zones and engage in some bonding fun.

Those otherwise stiff-laced Victorians were the inventors of many of the after-dinner games that still grace the drawing rooms and dinner tables of society today. Eating a cream cake with hands tied behind their backs or sitting on a friend's lap asking them to squeal provides a starkly contrasting Victorian image to the one we're familiar with, of public outcry at the flashing of ankles and shapely piano legs exposed to view, or the banning of conversation at dinner.

But by the 1850s the upper and middle classes were enjoying newly acquired leisure time and prosperity, and found themselves twiddling their thumbs as they'd run out of foreign lands to invade for Queen and Country. The old proverb 'Idle hands are the devil's playground' rings true, as this extended leisure time led a generation of young Victorian urbanites to develop a series of parlour games to amuse and entertain themselves at intimate gatherings.

Many of these kooky inventions form a requisite feature of family gatherings today. Queen Elizabeth II is said to favour the traditional team version of Charades at Windsor. My mother has been upholding In the Manner of the Word as an obligatory feature of Christmas as far back as I can remember.

The popularity of cooking shows and celebrity chefs is a reflection of our ever growing passion for all things gastronomic. As the nation gains culinary expertise, dinner parties have become a means of entertaining our friends without the restrictions and cost of going to a restaurant. As their popularity grows, so does the number of new and novel ways to entertain ourselves during the post-prandial lull.

The following chapters feature a reminder of how to play many of the Victorian classics, along with what I hope will offer some new games for you to enjoy and keep alive for future generations. The majority can be played at the table, but there are a few that require minor clearing or moving around. After-Dinner Organised Fun has been split into two chapters: one for those shorter games when you're looking for something to dip in and out of, and a second for those longer ones when you're signed up to settling in for the duration.

Human Buckaroo

What's the game?

This game can only be played when someone in your party has dozed off. They need to be pretty sound asleep – or, if they're Uncle Barry, drunk – to ensure they're not woken by the lightness of touch.

Remember the 1980s game Buckaroo? Well, this is the real life version.

What do I need to play it?

A large stack of empty plastic cups, and a sleeping guest.

How many friends?

At least two of you to play, and one sleeping victim.

How do I play it?

- Once you're certain that your victim is fast asleep, players each take a plastic cup and take it in turns to gently balance it somewhere on the sleeper. This must be done extremely carefully as the objective of the game is to not wake the victim up.
- Whoever is placing their cup when the sleeper wakes is the loser.

Race on Your Face

What's the game?

This had us in stitches when we played it around the dinner table one Christmas Eve. It was the sight of various family members pulling fantastically funny faces that provided the most entertainment. It's not ideal for teaching your children table manners but on one of those very long lunches where they have to stay in their seats it's a great way to keep them absorbed for a little bit longer.

What do I need to play it?

Something small and fairly flat per player, such as one of those biscuits for cheese or an after-dinner mint.

How many friends?

All the guests around the dinner table.

How do I play it?

- Players lean their heads back and each place the appointed item in the centre of their forehead. You might want an umpire to make sure that all items are positioned in the same place to prevent some players having an unfair advantage.

- On the word 'Go!' players race to get the item into their mouth by wrinkling and moving their face. If it falls off, the player has to place it back in the middle of their forehead and start again. First one to get the item in their mouth wins.

- There is a method to doing this, but if I tell you here it'll ruin the fun and give you an unfair advantage. Go figure it out.

Brough's Literary Telepathy

What's the game?

This game was invented and favoured by my boyfriend Barney's playful father. He delights at using it to befuddle new house guests and it's another obligatory feature of the family Christmas. You'll need an accomplice to play, but once you've got the hang of it, it's great to roll out again and again.

What do I need to play it?

Nine books and something to use as a pointy wand-like thing.

How many friends?

Great to play with two of you, but can easily befuddle a group.

How do I play it?

- Choose your accomplice and do this training bit in advance of playing the game, ideally out of sight of the other players.
- The object is to demonstrate your and your accomplice's telepathic powers by pretending to mind-read which book they've selected.
- Get yourself set up by laying your nine books out in a square.
- Before you start, you need to agree the non-verbal code you will use to communicate which book has been selected. The easiest way to do this is to use one of the books to represent the square of nine books by pointing to the area on the book that mirrors the location of the chosen book in the square of nine. If, for example, the chosen book is the one in the top left-hand corner, you point to the top left-hand corner of the single book.
- To fox the players, it's worth doing lots of elaborate wand-swishing, and as such you need to agree with your accomplice at which point you will reveal which book it is.
- When you're prepared, get your accomplice to go out of the room and

ask your guest to choose which book they'd like you to telepathically communicate to your accomplice.

- Next, get your accomplice to come back into the room and, after a bit of wafting and waving of the wand, touch one of the books in the place that represents where the chosen book is positioned.

- To ensure you don't give the game away, you might also want to touch multiple books in multiple places after you've done the first one.

- You then go through, pointing at the books in turn and asking 'Is it this one?' until you get to the correct one, where your accomplice appears to be able to read your mind by correctly identifying the book that your guest has selected.

- If you don't have any books to hand, you can just as easily replace them with any collection of nine objects.

Nine Nails Game

What's the game?

This is a great post-dinner focus to vex your guests as they try to figure out how to balance nine nails on one.

What do I need to play it?

Ten long nails with flat heads, with one of them banged into a log of wood.

How many friends?

A perfect challenge for one, or a focus for a small group.

How do I play it?

- Bang a nail into a log, pass this along with the nine other nails to your playing guests and ask them to figure out how to balance nine nails on one.
- It isn't a trick and there is a logical method.
- Don't read on if you want to try and figure it out yourself.
- Lay one of the nails on a steady surface and then lay seven of the remaining nails across it, alternating the direction they're facing, with the nail heads hooked over the first nail.
- Once done, lay the ninth nail on top of the first nail to hold them all in place.
- Next, pick up the first nail you laid down and lift it slowly, moving the other nails into place as they lock against the ninth nail.
- Once securely hanging in place, move over to the nail banged into the log and hang on top.

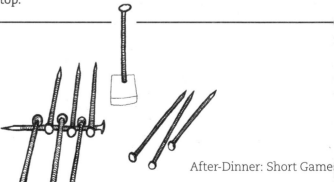

Up Jenkins

What's the game?

Up Jenkins is a very simple Victorian game of detection that works brilliantly after dinner. It's ideal to decide who's going to do the washing-up, as the forfeit for the losing team is banishment to the kitchen sink while the winners kick back and enjoy another game.

What do I need to play it?

A coin.

How many friends?

A nice full table – the more the merrier.

How do I play it?

- Split the table into two. The first team takes the coin and secretly passes it between themselves under the table, minimising movements or laying false movement clues as to the whereabouts of the coin.

- When someone on the opposing team knows where the coin is they shout 'Up Jenkins!' and point at the offending player, who must then stand up and reveal whether the coin is in their fist. If correct, the guessing team score a point, before handing the coin over for the other team to play.

- First team to five wins the pleasure of not doing the washing-up.

Charades

What's the game?

In any discussion of Victorian parlour games, Charades is nearly always the first to crop up as a suggestion. It was popularised by a 1980s TV series starring Una Stubbs and Lionel Blair that has arguably turned it into a cliché of itself, always eliciting a groan or two at its predictability whenever proposed. Such misfortune shouldn't banish it from your game-playing agenda, as its enduring entertainment value is what always made it so popular.

The game is believed to have originated in sixteenth-century France. It was later embraced by the Edwardians and the fun-loving Victorians as a permissible distraction. It also has a healthy literary pedigree, with Charlotte Brontë using it as a plot device in *Jane Eyre*. Other devotees include H. G. Wells and Peter Pan's creator J. M. Barrie, who were famed among friends as ambassadors for the game at social occasions. And we're apparently not the only primates to enjoy the game. Research by the University of St Andrews has suggested that apes are fans, too (9).

What do I need to play it?

Some pens and paper to write out the items to be mimed, and a hat per team to put them all in.

How many friends?

The game can be played individually if there's a small group of you, or in teams if there are lots.

How do I play it?

- These are the original rules for playing as a team. If you're playing individually, it's exactly the same, but players just come up with the charades at their turn.

- Give everyone a sheet of paper and a pen and get them to write out five charades. The charades should fall into the following six categories: books, plays, songs, films, television programmes and quotes. Once done, get everyone to tear out each one individually, fold them up and put them in the hat each team has been given, before passing the hat on to the next team.

After-Dinner: Short Games

- Each team then takes it in turn to act out the charade within sixty seconds. If they manage it, they get a point.

- The first team to go chooses their first player, who takes a slip of paper from the hat. They must now communicate to their team what the charade is without using words.

- First, they need to tell the team whether the item is a book, play, song, film, television series or quote. If, for example, the charade is *Harry Potter and the Goblet of Fire*, the player should perform the gestures for a book and a film.

- Next, they need to communicate how many words there are in the charade by holding up the corresponding number of fingers. They then select the word they're going to act out first by holding up the number of fingers corresponding to the position of the word in the phrase or title. To clarify this, the team's response to the acting might go something like: 'It's a film, it's got three words, this is the third word.'

- If the selected word is particularly long, you might choose to break it down into syllables and act out each syllable. To communicate this, you first tell your team how many syllables are in the word by holding the corresponding number of fingers on your upper arm, before following this up with the corresponding syllable that you're going to act out.

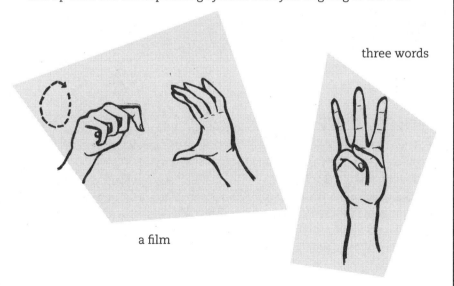

three words

a film

- There are also a number of legally allowed short cuts that you and your team need to know. To communicate 'the', simply create a T using your fingers, and to communicate a small word such as 'in', 'as', 'of', and so on, hold your forefinger and thumb up and get your team to reel the options off, ready for you to point and indicate when the right one has been discovered.

- Another short cut is to use 'sounds like'. Simply indicate which word or syllable you're going to act out, and then pull the bottom of your ear lobe or cup your hand round your ear to indicate the technique. So, for example, if it sounds like 'doors' (i.e. *Jaws*), you'd indicate the sequential word, which is of course the first one in this example, cup your ear, and then proceed to point at multiple doors in the room. If your team get 'door', you can get them to understand they need to extend it to 'doors' by facing your palms to each other and gently pulling them apart. The opposite can be used to indicate the shortening of a word.

- The first team to ten wins.

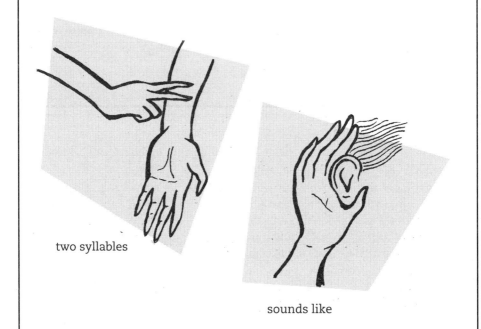

two syllables

sounds like

Silent Charades

What's the game?

This is an adaptation of the classic game of charades, but in this format the whole game is performed without words. It's relatively quick and a good one to play after dinner to cajole guests into the idea of an evening of game-playing fun.

What do I need to play it?

Some pens and paper, and a hat to put the slips of paper in.

How many friends?

This can only be played with a minimum of eight people and you need to have even numbers to make it work. The larger the group the better.

How do I play it?

- To start, split the group into two and get one of the teams to come up with and write out two copies of a charade each. As with the traditional game, the charade must be either a book, play, song, film, television programme or quote.

- Next, collect both copies of each of the charades together in a hat and, once done, take it and pass it around both groups, getting everyone to take a slip of paper out.

- On the word 'Go!' all players must act out the charade on their piece of paper while simultaneously looking around the room to find who else is acting out the same charade as them.

- As soon as they spot their charade partner they must indicate their recognition to their partner and both sit down. The last pair to sit down are out. All pairs then take it in turns to read out their charade, and if they're mismatched, they're also out.

- Repeat the game until the last remaining pair in is the winner.

The Wizard of Swerford

What's the game?

This is another game courtesy of Barney's dad, who used to live in an Oxfordshire village in a house called Swerford. It's an ingenious card stunt designed to be played anywhere in the world. You just need a pre-briefed sidekick who knows what to do whenever you call and ask 'Is the Wizard of Swerford available?'

What do I need to play it?

A pack of cards.

How many friends?

You, your sidekick on the end of a telephone and a few other friends to be bemused and impressed.

How do I play it?

- The idea of the game is to befuddle your friends into thinking you know a mind-reading wizard.

- To play, get one of your friends to choose a card from the pack, then look at it yourself before announcing that you're going to call the Wizard of Swerford to get him or her to read your mind as to what the card is.

- Next, call your accomplice who will be fully briefed on the following routine.

- When they answer, say 'Hello, is the Wizard of Swerford available?' at which point your accomplice knows that they need to immediately start reciting the different card suits. As they say 'Spades, diamonds, clubs and hearts,' you carry on as if you're having a conversation, for example, 'Oh really, are you? I hear it's beautiful around this time of the year.'

- When your accomplice hits the correct suit you confirm this but make it appear that it's part of the conversation: 'Yes, yes, that's right, we did go there in June.' By doing this, your accomplice knows which is the suit. They then need to communicate the number of the selected card.

- The same process is played out with the accomplice reciting the card numbers and you blithely confirming when they hit the right one: 'Yes, OK, I'll pass the message on then.'

- You then say to your accomplice that you're going to pass them on to a friend and that they're to mind read which card they have selected.

- Your friend is passed the phone and your accomplice has moved into the role of the Wizard of Swerford and correctly identifies which card has been selected.

Call My Bluff

What's the game?

If some of the earlier games are too banal for you, Call My Bluff is a more relaxed and generally more civilised option. The game requires players to draft an effective fake dictionary definition, so any youngsters at the table might need a helping hand.

What do I need to play it?

A dictionary, pens and paper.

How many friends?

At least three of you.

How do I play it?

- Players take it in turns to lead each round. Each leader chooses an obscure word from the dictionary, one which they're fairly certain no one knows the definition of.

- All the guests need to write a plausible definition for the word. The objective of the game is to confuse other players into selecting yours as the correct one. If you have an inkling of what the actual definition is, then write this out as if correct. It'll earn you extra points.

- When done, everyone anonymously submits them to the holder of the dictionary. The dictionary holder needs to write out the actual definition on another slip of paper to prevent players easily guessing the correct one.

- Each definition is then read out by the leader and players must guess which is the right one. Scoring is as follows:
  - All players choosing the actual definition get two points.
  - Players also get a point for each person who selects the definition they wrote.
  - If no one identifies the correct definition then the leader of that round gets a point.
  - If someone has written a definition that is close to the real one, that person also gets two points.
- The game then moves on with different people leading each round. Once everyone has had a go, the player with the highest score wins.
- NB: It's hugely important that everyone writes as clearly as possible, as if a player can't read someone else's writing when it's their turn to read the definition out, then they're likely to give away the fact that it's not the actual one.

Wink Murder

What's the game?

A game of little effort involving death by winking.

What do I need to play it?

Paper and a pen.

How many friends?

More than three but hard to play with over twenty.

How do I play it?

- First off, write out a piece of paper for every player, ensuring you have one M for 'murderer' and a D for 'detective', with the rest of the pieces featuring a V for 'victim'.
- Put all the pieces in a hat and get everyone to pick one out.
- If you're the detective then your objective is to spot the killer; if you're the murderer it's to kill everyone by the evil wink of your eye; and if you're a victim then you die a blood-curdling death as soon as someone winks at you.
- The game ends when the detective spots who the murderer is. Repeat the game. The winner is the detective who manages to spot the murderer with the fewest victims.
- First player to five wins the pleasure of not doing the washing-up.

Waiter Stunt

What's the game?

This is much less of a game but more a trick to play on a food-loving friend when you next go out for dinner. Not for after dinner as such, but more an eating out pre-dinner activity. It works particularly well if played on someone who prides themselves on their passion for and knowledge of food. You know the sort of person I mean: the one that's prone to gout.

What do I need to play it?

A waiter who's up for playing along.

How many friends?

However many of you are out for dinner.

How do I play it?

- On arrival at the restaurant find out who your waiter is and see if they're up for coming in on the gag. If they are, you need to brief them that when the selected member of your party orders, they must look at them incredulously and ask 'Are you sure?', as if they've just made an enormous gastronomic gaffe.

- The rest of the party must also be briefed in advance to agree with waiter and look mildly shocked when the victim looks around for support.

- It's up to you as to when you let them know you've been playing a joke on them. I imagine it will depend on how well they take it.

Bladder Wars

What's the game?

The loser is the first person to have to go to the toilet. Invented by my boyfriend, not me. Its saving grace is that it's great to prevent a hangover as it allows you to rehydrate.

What do I need to play it?

Shot glasses and several jugs or bottles of water.

How many friends?

As many as you like.

How do I play it?

Players match each other shot for shot of water. First one to the toilet loses.

The Shaving Game

What's the game?

This is a game of trust where players demonstrate their shaving prowess. Men will obviously be at an advantage, though it's a different ball game when you're shaving someone else.

What do I need to play it?

Shaving or squirty cream, and a cloth for each of the shavers to wipe their cream onto. A blunt knife (or plastic spoon) and blindfold for each pair.

How many friends?

As many pairs as you like.

How do I play it?

- Start off pairing people up as teams (male and female, husbands and wives, girlfriends and boyfriends will work).
- One of the pair sits down while the other is blindfolded, and then applies shaving cream to the seated player's face.
- Once prepared, the blindfolded player continues by attempting to shave their partner using a plastic knife or similar implement.
- The person who did the best job within the set time period wins.

Name That Song

What's the game?

This is a test of musical knowledge. The objective is to think of a song with a certain word in the title or lyrics.

What do I need to play it?

Just yourselves.

How many friends?

Ideal for two or more players.

How do I play it?

- Decide who's going first and get them to choose a word (ideally not too hard at the beginning), and the other players have to think of a song that features that word.

- Whoever gets it first gets a point, and it's then their turn to choose a word.

- If the group can't think of a song that features the word that's been put forward, they shout out 'Challenge!' and the person who came up with the word has to sing the song line they were thinking of that features that word. If they sing it correctly, they get a point and another go. If the challenged player can't sing a song line featuring their nominated word, they lose a point.

Fizz Buzz

What's the game?

You might argue on first read that this one should be confined to the maths class. Strangely, it is brilliant to play with friends and only requires a very basic grasp of the times table.

What do I need to play it?

Some sort of forfeit device, if you decide to play with forfeits. This is probably best known as a drinking game, but you could use a points system instead, where points are awarded for each mess-up and chores assigned to the person with the most. Alternatively, come up with some embarrassing things that players have to do, for example swapping clothes with the person sat opposite or trying to sing a song while gargling water.

How many friends?

You could play it with two of you, but great to play in a medium-sized group.

How do I play it?

- Get everyone to sit in a circle and then take it in turns to count, so the first player would say 'One', the next would say 'Two', and so on.
- When a player gets to a number that is divisible by three they must say, 'Fizz', and when they reach one that's divisible by five they must say, 'Buzz', so, for example: 'One', 'Two', 'Fizz', 'Four', 'Buzz', 'Fizz' . . .
- If playing with points, everyone starts with five and then loses one each time they get it wrong until they have no points left and they're out. Alternatively, you can use drinks as forfeits for mathematical errors.

Amaretti Biscuit Wrapper Lanterns

What's the game?

An impressive after-dinner stunt and a welcome return to indoor fireworks since the European Union banished them to the dustbins of history. This one came out of long, lazy lunches over Christmas when yummy, tasty amaretti biscuits were served, wrapped in those thin paper sheets. Call it reckless, but this game involves setting light to bits of paper and letting them fly around the room. All usual recommendations of employing common sense apply, along with a suggestion not to play in a thatched cottage if you're anywhere near the rafters.

What do I need to play it?

A tin of those amaretti biscuits that are individually wrapped in paper.

How many friends?

As many as are around the table.

How do I play it?

- Unwrap one of the biscuits, flatten out the wrapper and make it into a neat cylinder.
- Light the top rim as evenly as possible, stand back and let it fly.
- As the display burns out it will fall to the ground in a ball of ash.
- On second thoughts, play this one in the garden.

Cake Race

What's the game?

I still struggle to believe it, but this was a Victorian favourite played out in parlours throughout the period. It's hard to imagine such base and disgraceful table manners and outright gorging taking place even today, but if the Victorians approved of it, it can't be all that bad. You might find that kids have a natural propensity for this game.

What do I need to play it?

A cake cut into equal portions for each player, and something to tie everyone's hands behind their backs.

How many friends?

However many slices of cake you have, or vice versa. Essentially, it's great for any number.

How do I play it?

- Cut up and distribute your cake.
- Tie your dinner guests' arms behind their backs and ask them to consume their cake using only their mouths.
- If you want to take it to the Victorian finale, then the winner is the one who licks their plate, picks it up with their teeth and manages to drop it over their head behind them. I'd suggest using plastic plates to prevent an even greater mess than is necessary.

Consequences

What's the game?

This is another Victorian parlour game that has been adapted into many forms. One of my favourites is the verbal version (see Walkie Talkie in Chapter One: Organised Fun for the Great Outdoors). The original version involves players taking it in turns to write a line without seeing the one the previous player has written.

What do I need to play it?

Paper and a pen per player.

How many friends?

Between four and eight is the ideal number to ensure there isn't too much time in between each go.

How do I play it?

- Give every player a sheet of paper and a pen and get them each to write one or more sequential adjectives on the top, then fold the paper so the writing is concealed and get everyone to pass it to their right-hand neighbour.
- Next, everyone writes the name of a man before folding and passing on as before. This writing, folding and passing continues with the following:
  - 'Met . . .' and then the name of a woman.
  - Where they met.
  - What he gave her.
  - What he said to her.
  - What she said to him.
  - The consequence of this.
  - And, lastly, what the world said about it.

- When everyone's done, the papers are collected in and the host reads each one out. An example might be:

  The sickeningly vile Father Christmas met Mrs Tiddlewinkle on the beach in Hawaii. He gave her a pair of fire billows and said to her, 'Never take things off strange men.' She said to him, 'I've always hankered after a pair of stripy pyjamas with my initials embroidered on them.' The consequence was that she caused a mass arranged marriage of anyone with a B in their surname. The world said they were filled with sublimity and delight.

- You can of course substitute the categories to something bespoke to your group. The words are your oyster.

Button and Funnel

What's the game?

Yet another surprisingly crass Victorian jape. You need two gullible guests who can take a joke. Best played in the summer and when the victims have a change of clothes to hand.

What do I need to play it?

Two buttons, two plastic funnels and two glasses of water. You need two victims to prevent one of them feeling picked-on and to make them feel as though it's a race.

How many friends?

Two victims, and however many players you like.

How do I play it?

- Ask your two victims to stick the pipe end of a funnel down the front of their trousers and balance a button on their foreheads. They then race to see who's the first to manage to get the button from their foreheads and into the funnel that's tucked into their waistbands.
- While the victims are fully engaged in their task, two others step forward and tip a glass of water down each funnel.
- Step back and hope they've got a sense of humour.

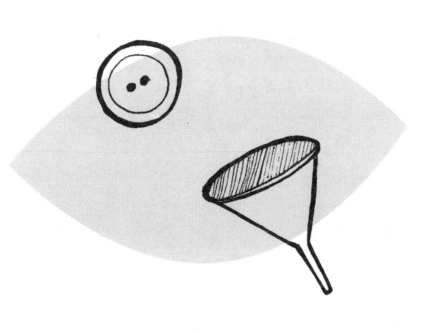

FIVE

After-Dinner Organised Fun: Longer Games

There are a few ingredients that are vital to creating the perfect occasion for a prolonged session of organised fun. Firstly, you need to have had a very large and ideally late lunch or early dinner. The main part of the consumption should have been wrapped up by at least 8 p.m. – too early for guests to go home or the children to bed, but too late for someone to suggest a walk or similar distraction.

Secondly, you want the group to have either moved from the dinner table to the sofas, or at least have settled themselves in comfortably. Shoes should be off and belts undone to allow the stomach to get stuck into its digesting, thus calling for an alternative stimulus to prevent guests squabbling or dozing off.

The following chapter features a collection of ideas to engage and absorb you, to create a magical afternoon extending into a long evening of bonding fun.

Theatrical Chinese Whispers

What's the game?

This game was invented by my siblings and cousins after boring our parents rigid with incessant demands to play Chinese Whispers at our dinner table. By bending the rules slightly we liberated ourselves from our seats.

What do I need to play it?

Hardly anything, but if you want to go to town you can bring in all sorts of props.

How many friends?

Definitely more than three of you.

How do I play it?

- The group splits into two teams.
- Team A goes out of the room and Team B thinks of an action or sequence of actions – as mundane or as dramatic as you choose – for example, pruning the roses or winning the Grand National.
- One member of Team A returns to the room. The sequence is acted out in front of them by a member of Team B.
- Another member of Team A then returns to the room.
- The first member of Team A then needs to act out their interpretation of what they've seen to their team member.
- And so the sequence goes on, until the last team member enters the room, sees the sequence acted out and has to guess what the performance is about.
- The game then plays on, with the other team going outside.

Dough You Know
What It Is?

What's the game?

If you're bored of the classic game of Charades and fancy something a little different, this one's a great alternative and, to my mind, a whole lot more amusing. Some friends and their kids came and stayed with us one weekend and the kids brought along their play dough, a soft, clay-like substance that doesn't go hard when you make shapes out of it. We were taking it in turns to demonstrate our sculpting ability when it occurred to us that there was a brilliant game in this.

What do I need to play it?

Ideally, you need a different colour play dough for each team. If you're struggling to get your hands on any, you can make some salt dough which works in the same way. Simply mix together three cups of flour, one cup of salt, four cups of water and one tablespoon of glycerine (available from chemists or supermarkets). You can then add food colouring so that each team has a different colour.

The easy alternative is to use Blu-tac. You'll also need some pens and paper and a hat or pan to put the slips of paper into.

How many friends?

Works for small- to medium-sized groups of between four and twelve.

How do I play it?

- The object of the game is to be the first team to communicate a word through sculpting it out of dough for their teammates to guess.
- To start off, you need to get one person to write out ten things for each of the players in the game. Make sure that all suggestions are feasible to sculpt out of dough. Put these in a hat or pan in the middle of the table.
- Next, get yourselves into teams. The ideal number in each team is three, but as long as there are more than one you can make it work.

- Everyone takes it in turns to be the dough sculptor for the team. Decide who's going first, and that person pulls a slip of paper out of the hat, looks at it and then passes it on to the other player in each team whose turn it is to sculpt.
- On the word 'Go!' the sculptor in each team simultaneously starts squeezing, crafting and shaping their dough to somehow communicate what the word is. It's up to you whether you allow animation of the dough – animating the bird so it flies through the sky by waving it around in the air, for example.
- The very clear rule, however, is that communication must be through the dough model and any other sort of body action is not allowed.
- The first team to guess correctly wins a point. The first team to ten points wins.

Ellie's Brilliant Name Game

What's the game?

This is a guaranteed hit for any occasion and will have people engrossed for a good couple of hours. It's my wonderful friend Ellie's favourite game and is traditionally rolled out at her family Christmas each year. Another winning alternative to Charades.

What do I need to play it?

A hat, pens and paper.

How many friends?

Two or more – no limits, but it might get a bit boring waiting for your turn if there are quite a few of you.

How do I play it?

- Get everyone to split into two teams.
- Each player tears a piece of paper into between five and ten small pieces (depending on how long you want the game to go on for) and writes the name of a famous person on each piece – fictional or real.
- All pieces of paper are then put into a hat/saucepan/colander/whatever in the middle of the table.
- The first team to start chooses a player, who takes a piece of paper from the bowl and describes the person on the paper to the rest of their team without mentioning their name. They can do anything but say the name on the paper. Impressions and 'sounds like' clues are allowed.
- They continue doing this for one minute, describing as many names as they can get through. If their team guesses correctly, that name goes into a small pile. If they can't get it, it goes back in the hat. At the end of the sixty seconds, the number of correct guesses are counted and this is the score for that team. Pieces of paper that have been correctly guessed are put in a separate bowl.

- It's then someone on the next team's turn and the game plays on, swapping between teams until all the names have been used up.

- The game then goes into round two, and the same process is gone through again, using the same names as before, but this time team members are only allowed to say one word to enable others to try and guess what it is. For example, if the character was Marilyn Monroe and it was mentioned in the previous round that 'she was the film star in that famous shot where she's stood on the grille with her skirt blowing up', then you might choose to just say 'Skirt.'

- In the final round players have to mime each character, hoping that their teammates remember each one from the two previous rounds.

- The team with the highest score wins.

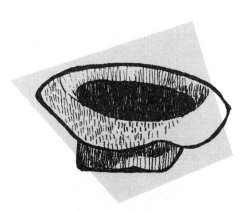

Kate's Drawing Game

What's the game?

You might be fooled into thinking artistic types will have an advantage in this game, but their attention to the aesthetic is in fact a hindrance. If you can hold a pencil you can play this. Barney's aunt Kate devised the format for this game one Christmas. Teams have to guess the word their team member is drawing. Brilliant for big, boisterous groups, but easily scaled down too.

What do I need to play it?

Some pens and paper.

How many friends?

Great for groups large and small.

How do I play it?

- First of all, you need a list of subjects to draw. I'd suggest coming up with words around four themes, for example food, films, history and so on. You can get as obscure or as personal as you like. A section on Granddad's bad habits might be interesting. As you write your list, you need to be sure that your words aren't too 'out there' or, more importantly, too hard to draw.

- Split everyone into two teams (or even more if you're playing in a large group), send them off into separate rooms and position yourself somewhere in a room that's equidistant between them.

- On the word 'Go!' players on each team take it in turns to race out to you, each be given the same word and race back to draw it out for their team members, who have to guess what it is. Players mustn't speak (obviously), mime or write down the word. Only drawing is allowed. It's up to you whether players can draw an ear for 'sounds like'.

- As soon as they guess correctly, another player races out to get the next word from you before racing back and drawing it.

- The first team to draw out all of the words correctly wins.

- If you're a little concerned about how trustworthy each player is, then I'd suggest having an umpire who sits in each room to ensure no cheating.

The Stool of Repentance

What's the game?

Not, you'll be relieved to hear, a Victorian game to be played on the toilet, but rather one for the parlour. In this one you take it in turns to be accused of a crime by your friends before guessing who's trying to pin it on you.

What do I need to play it?

A stool for the victim to stand on and a pen and paper for the 'judge' to write down the accused crime.

How many friends?

Great for a medium-sized group of between six and ten.

How do I play it?

- Someone starts off as the 'accused', another of you plays the 'judge' and the remainder are the 'jury'.

- The jury sit in a semicircle facing the accused, who stands on a chair with the judge beside him or her.

- The game begins with the judge saying, 'Illustrious jury, do each of you know why [name of victim] has been brought here before us?' To which the jury answers, 'Yes.'

- Each juror then takes it in turns to come up and whisper the accused crime in the judge's ear, who scribbles each one down to help him or her remember them. I'd suggest scribbling the crimes down in a different order to prevent the accused guessing who nominated each one. One crime might be that the accused doesn't put the lid back on the toothpaste, or arguably a more serious accusation could be that they assassinated the prime minister and are trying to pin it on their dog.

- Once all are collected, the judge reads each one out and the accused has to guess who accused them of which crime.

- If the accused correctly guesses who came up with a crime, they then swap places with the juror who wrote it, and so the game plays on.

The Book Game

What's the game?

This game should appeal to the literati. It's perfect to play if you've hired a holiday cottage, as they frequently have an eclectic and often comedic collection of books that past house guests have left behind.

What do I need to play it?

A selection of books – include some obscure ones for added interest – and a pad and pen per player.

How many friends?

At least three of you.

How do I play it?

- Put the selection of books in the centre of the table and ensure each player has a pad and pen.
- Players take it in turns to lead a round, with each selecting a book and reading out the title, blurb and author's name.
- The rest of the players must then write the most convincing first line. The objective of the game is to dupe the rest of the players into thinking yours is the right one.
- Whoever is leading the round must also write down the actual first line before collecting everyone else's in and adding theirs to the pile.
- The leader then takes each one and reads them out in turn as convincingly as possible.
- Players must guess which one they think is correct.

- Points are awarded as follows:
  - If someone chooses a fake line, the person who wrote that line gets one point.
  - Two points if someone guesses the right line.
  - If nobody picks the true first line then the person who is leading that round scores two points.
  - Finally, players get five points if they write the correct first line for the book. It sounds unlikely but it has happened!
- The game moves around with each person taking it in turn to read.
- NB: As with Call My Bluff, everyone needs to write clearly as possible, as if a player can't decipher the writing when they read the lines out it will be obvious that it's a fake.

The Name Game

What's the game?

Amazingly, since I first encountered this as The Rizla Game as a teenager, this actually turns out to be another of those delightful Victorian parlour games. It's synonymous with my time at university as it was the perfect distraction to our studies and helped fill lecture-free hours and late-night sessions.

What do I need to play it?

A packet of Rizlas (the larger ones are the best) and some pens to write on them.

How many friends?

Best played with more than three.

How do I play it?

- Everyone chooses a character – fictional or real, living or dead – and writes the character's name on a Rizla, before sticking it to the forehead of the person sat next to them without them seeing it. I'd suggest asking the person to lick and stick it themselves as the thought of someone else's saliva festering on your forehead is a mild distraction to the game.

- Players must then ask the group a 'yes or no' question to help them guess who they are. The other players are not allowed to say anything other than 'Yes' or 'No'.

- If they get the question right they're allowed to ask another one. If they get it wrong then it moves on to the next person's go.

- The loser is obviously the last one out.

In the Manner of the Word

What's the game?

This is my mum's favourite game and one that is an obligatory part of the proceedings at every family Christmas. Being the mildly extrovert character that she is, I'm sure it has something to do with the fact that she's able to fling herself about as she throws herself into a missed dramatic calling. Great for budding actors, it's easy to explain and just as easy to pick up. A winner for the whole family.

What do I need to play it?

Nothing.

How many friends?

Ideal for groups of four to ten.

How do I play it?

- Decide who's first to go, get them to step outside the room and close the door to ensure they're well out of earshot.

- Meanwhile, the rest of the players whisper together to decide which adverb they'd like to play out on this round. You might choose 'disarmingly', for example, or if you're playing with kids try something a bit simpler such as 'grumpily' or 'hungrily'. Make sure you choose an adverb that the player outside the room will understand, but equally one that's challenging enough.

- Once it's decided, the player is called back in. They must then choose someone and ask them to do something 'in the manner of the word'. For example, if the word was 'regally' and the selected player was asked to bake a cake in the manner of the word, they might choose to smatter their cake-baking performance with a few royal waves, or ensure they take off and polish their crown before rolling up their royal sleeves to ice the cake.

- As soon as the player has guessed the correct adverb, they swap with whoever's performance helped them guess, and it's that person's turn to go out of the room.

Crambo

What's the game?

There are a number of variations to this ancient game. There's the simple rhyming version where players take it in turns to find another word that rhymes with the word just spoken (great for kids); the slightly more complicated version where players take it in turns to come up with the next line to a poem, paying due observation to metre and rhyme; and finally the version written here, which I think has the broadest appeal and works well for an evening with adults or an afternoon of games with the family.

What do I need to play it?

Nothing.

How many friends?

A group of between four and ten is ideal.

How do I play it?

- Choose someone to go out of the room and the remaining party must choose a word for that person to guess. The selected word must have a number of other words that sound like it, such as 'pen', 'take', or 'thing'.
- When the player outside comes back into the room they are given a word that sounds like the one that has been chosen. For example, if the chosen word is 'fate' then they might be told that a similar word is 'late'.
- The player then must proceed to guess what the word is by asking a question along the lines of, 'Is it a girl's name?' The remaining party must then answer, 'No, it's not Kate.'
- These questions and answers play on until the correct word is guessed, at which point another player steps outside to take their turn.

Dumb Crambo

What's the game?

Dumb Crambo is a more energetic version of Crambo (see opposite), where all words are substituted by acting.

What do I need to play it?

Nothing.

How many friends?

A group of between four and ten is ideal.

How do I play it?

- The game is played as before, but when the person comes back into the room one of the remaining party acts out a word that sounds like the chosen word. So, for example, if the chosen word was 'kite', they might act out 'fight'.

- The player who was outside must then act out a series of words that sound like the one they've identified. Instead of speaking, the gathered party must boo or hiss when the answer is incorrect, and leap to their feet cheering when the correct one is finally identified.

Personalities

What's the game?

This is a favourite of many families I know. It appeals to all ages and gets everyone moving around, preventing anyone falling into a post-feast coma. The game involves players choosing a character and then in teams trying to guess who each other is. The ultimate aim is to make the other players join your family team.

What do I need to play it?

Paper and pens.

How many friends?

Great for big groups. Can't be played with fewer than eight.

How do I play it?

- The objective of the game is to guess the personalities that other players have given themselves.

- Nominate one games leader and then divide into families of between three and five, depending on how many people are playing. Get each family team to position themselves in different corners of the room.

- Next, everyone decides on a character without telling anyone else, and they scribble it down on a slip of paper (it could be Charlie Chaplin, Tom Cruise, the Queen or David Beckham, for example). Give the names to the games leader, who puts them in a hat. It's important that players choose characters they know everyone will know, and they should also think of avoiding a personality that's too obviously them. The idea is to fox other players away from guessing who each of you are.

- Once collected, the games leader reads the full list aloud twice. If you want to be strict about it you can make this once. All players must attempt to memorise the names.

- The aim of the game is to guess who is which personality, with the winner being the person who is the last to be guessed.

- The first team tries to guess the character of someone on the opposite team. To do this you should try and think what sort of character that person might choose to be. For example, if your aunt has a Beatrix Potter fetish then you might conclude that she's Jemima Puddle-Duck, unless you think someone has chosen it as a red herring.

- When a team makes a correct guess, the player they have identified moves over to join their group. The team keeps on guessing the other players' identities until they get one wrong and it then moves to the next team to take up the challenge.

- If the other team have been playing correctly, they will have listened to the identities of all the players that were called over and will then call them back and hopefully add a couple more.

- The game plays on in this way until one team has everybody there. The winner is the last person left who hasn't been identified.

Slap My Yodel

What's the game?

This game came from a skiing trip in the Austrian mountains and is an adaptation of one I picked up on my travels. The first time we played it was with a mixed group of English, German and Swiss friends. Towards the end of the game the English were the only ones left playing and rolling around at the hilarity of it all, while our European compadres stared on in bemusement.

What do I need to play it?

A forfeit for losing players. If children are playing, give everyone five points at the start, one of which is then deducted each time someone messes up. If only adults are playing, you could introduce a drinking forfeit. You also need to be sitting at a table.

How many friends?

Great for groups of between six and twelve. Any more and it can get a bit boring waiting for your turn.

How do I play it?

- Get everyone to sit in a circle around a table with their hands placed in front of them. Next, get everyone to lift their left hand and cross it over the arm of the person to their left.

- The first person to go slaps the table and the person to their left slaps the table using the hand that is lying to the left of the one that did the last table slap. The slapping must then progress around the table in an unbroken circle. This sounds easy, but because your arms are crossed, it gets very confusing, particularly when the pressure is on.

- A player can confuse things by choosing to slap the table twice at any moment. This sends the slapping in the opposite direction. If someone chooses to slap the table three times during the game, the player next to them according to the order of play has to stand up and yodel, before sitting back down and sending the table slap around in the same direction as before.
- If someone gets it wrong, they get a forfeit or lose a point.
- The idea is that the table slapping speeds up as the play goes on, causing complication and confusion as people fail to keep track of what's going on.
- You can add further actions depending on how complicated you want to make it. Alternatively, if you're playing in a really big group you can start another slap on the opposite side, meaning that players have two games they have to watch.

Louis's Beer Pong

What's the game?

This is hugely popular with American students and is played out in campuses across the States. It's also a favourite among bar staff in the UK as a means of divvying up tips at the end of the night.

What do I need to play it?

An oblong table, thirty-two empty plastic or paper cups, two ping-pong balls and some beer if you want to introduce a drinking element to the game.

How many friends?

Best played with two pairs, or one-on-one.

How do I play it?

- Each player lines up sixteen cups to create a ten-cup triangle with six cups balanced on top.

- If you want to introduce the drinking element then put some beer in each of the cups.

- Players then take it in turns to stand at opposite ends of the table and shoot the ping-pong ball so that it lands in one of their opponents' cups. Players can either use a straight lob, or as you get good at it you might decide to introduce a bounce, which makes it slightly harder.

- If successful, the opposing team has to drink from the cup containing the ball, and this cup is then removed from play. If the drinking element is not included, the cup is simply moved out of the way.

- The winning team is the team to remove all their opponents' cups from the table.

Rookwood Tantrums

What's the game?

Rookwood Tantrums was invented by my mother, father and beloved aunt Mary Rose, who late one summer evening concocted a card game with a melodramatic twist. The object of the game is to get rid of your cards as quickly as possible. Whoever is the first to do this collects all the monies in the pot.

What do I need to play it?

A pack of cards and some small change.

How many friends?

Ideal for smaller groups of three or four.

How do I play it?

- The aim of the game is to get rid of your cards as quickly as possible and avoid paying any penalties along the way (more explained later). If it looks as though a penalty is due, players have the option to throw a tantrum, and if the performance is deemed suitably dramatic then the other players can decide to let you off.
- To get started, take a full pack of cards and deal them out to all players.
- Whoever is holding the aces lays them on the playing table, facing upwards.
- There are two types of money on the table in this game: the 'ace bet' and the 'common pot'. The common pot is the stack of cash in the middle of the table into which players pay their fines. The ace bet is the amount of money that is stipulated at the beginning of the game and is placed on top of each of the aces.
- The dealer then stipulates the ace bet. Those who have laid down aces are obliged to place the nominated bet on each ace. The minimum ace bet can be nothing.
- In addition to the ace bet, each player places an agreed sum (the common penalty) into the common pot. That bet is then consistent for all games.

- The dealer changes at each game in a clockwise direction.
- The player who will be next to deal plays first, and thereafter play continues in a clockwise direction.
- To play Rookwood Tantrums, each player takes their turn to lay a card down on the corresponding suit in numerical downward order, i.e. king, queen, jack and so on, with the two card always being placed last.
- If a player is unable to play, then that player misses a turn and pays a penalty into the common pot. At this point the player has the option to throw a tantrum if they can't go. (Rules apply. See tantrum notes below.)
- For those players who have a two (the last possible card in any suit), a secondary objective exists, namely to play that card: the player who plays a two wins any ace bet monies associated with that suit.
- At the end of the game, any ace bet monies not won are carried over to the next game and put in the common pot.
- The winner of the final game wins the common pot of cash and any ace bet monies not won during that game.
- Tantrum notes: players also have the option to choose not to pay a fine, but to throw a tantrum instead. Any 'tantrum players' must adhere to the following rules:
  1. Tantrum players must declare themselves at the beginning of the game.
  2. Such tantrum players are obliged to double the official stake into the common pot.
  3. If, during the course of play, a tantrum player is unable to play a card, then payment of penalty into the common pot can be avoided by throwing a tantrum.
  4. Before throwing a tantrum, a player must stipulate the nature of the tantrum to be thrown, namely a Common Tantrum, Royal Tantrum or a Right Royal Tantrum.
  5. To achieve a tantrum of any of these definitions, the back must be in contact with the floor at all times.
  6. It is illegal for an object to be taken to the floor by players throwing a tantrum.

Mafia

What's the game?

The Russians were the inventors of this parody of the underworld. They apparently play it in schools and universities as a way of educating children about the political system of the country. The game can be incredibly long and complex, so for simplicity's sake I've included the most basic format. There are lots of variations that can be introduced and multiple books, websites and online versions of the game. I'll leave you to master this one before embarking on some of your own investigations on where to take it next.

What do I need to play it?

A deck of cards and some time, patience and willing players.

How many friends?

Works best in groups of between four and ten.

How do I play it?

- The aim of the game is to be the last surviving player. The game involves 'mafia' voting to kill 'townspeople', and the townspeople choosing which mafia player to lynch. The mafia will be happily helping to kill off a colleague if it helps save their bacon. The key to the game if you're a mafia player is to keep cool and master the art of bluffing. If you're a townsperson it's all about detecting when another player is lying.

- Get yourself set up so that you're all sat where you can see each other. Decide who is going to be the 'mayor', who is in effect the moderator. Ideally, it should be someone who knows the rules and has played the game before.

- Next, prepare your cards to decide who's going to be which character. The number of each type of character depends on players' preferences for game length. An easy method for calculating how many mafia you need is to have one mafia for every two non-mafia players.

- Based on the number of people playing and using the mafia member formula above, prepare your cards so that there's one card per person.

Use a card from the black suits (clubs and spades) to denote who will be the mafia and include the relevant number of black cards based on the formula described above, and also put one queen in there for the mayor. The rest of the pack is made up from red cards to denote townspeople. Everyone draws a card to find out which role they are playing.

- The game is then played through night and day sequences until either the mafia have been eliminated, or the number of mafia and townspeople is equal, in which case the mafia win.

- To get started, you enter the night sequence where everyone closes their eyes. The mayor will instruct only members of the mafia to open their eyes, to acknowledge each other, before closing them again.

- Next, the mayor tells all players to open their eyes and you enter the day sequence. All players must now debate among each other as to who they think is the mafia; this requires some good bluffing work on the part of the mafia. Players must all decide who they think is the mafia before voting, with the exception of the accused, who needs to be protesting their innocence in an attempt to save their life. Once a unanimous decision is made, that player is then voted 'dead'.

- Once dead, they reveal what their role actually was and they're then out of the game. It's crucial that players who are dead do not speak during the rest of the game, as they might give away some vital clues as they watch the proceedings in full view.

- Night falls again and the mayor asks everyone to close their eyes. The mayor says the names of all players and the mafia need to vote on who they would like to kill next by raising their hand (while still keeping their eyes closed) when that person's name is read out. The townsperson with the highest number of votes is then dead.

- The next day begins with the mayor asking everyone to open their eyes before announcing last night's victim. The game then moves into the day sequence as before.

- The game plays on, moving through the night and day sequences as described above. The townspeople win when they eliminate all the members of the mafia. The mafia wins if there are equal numbers of mafia and townspeople left.

SIX

Organised Fun for Later in the Evening

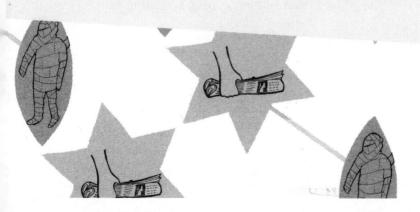

There will always be someone who'll be against the idea of a game. While everyone bounds around with enthusiasm and suggestions, there'll be a naysayer among the group providing a backdrop of grumbling as they shuffle to the corner, cross-armed and grumpy-faced.

When we were younger, my brother used to perform the Grinch role in our family. It was around the time he'd hit adolescence, when his new teenage perspective cast such antics as cringingly uncool.

There's often also an old faithful in a group of familiar friends. At the slightest murmur of a game you can see them sloping back to the sofa, head hung like a turtle, chin slumped in hand. The inevitability of such proceedings means that they'll reluctantly partake in the end, and will soon be found leaping around and shouting their enthusiasm with the best of them.

It's the lively games in this chapter that fill those grumps with fear. The thought of such uninhibited game playing is akin to arriving at a party and realising you forgot to get dressed. But once shaken off the comfortable sofa, they'll soon be joining you in the joy of abandon and the life-affirming pleasure that can be gained from some bonding, bounding fun.

Toilet-Paper Mummies

What's the game?

I'm not quite sure what the element of appeal is, but this is one of my favourites. It sounds ridiculous when described, but bear with me and give it a go. We've played it on New Year's Eve when it's gone down a storm, but it's also been a bit of a damp squib when guests weren't at the jovial, genial stage of the evening. For those conscious of wasting valuable resources, you can wind your toilet roll back up for use, but be warned: you are left with an inelegant pile of unhygienic bottom-wiping material.

What do I need to play it?

Toilet rolls. One for each team.

How many friends?

As many teams as you like, though ideally no more than three in each team.

How do I play it?

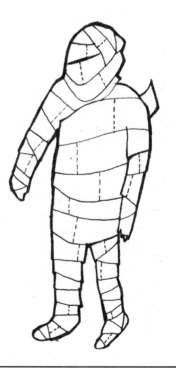

- Split players into teams of three and give each team a toilet roll.

- Decide who's the 'Egyptian mummy' and stand them in the middle between the other two players. Those two players then wrap the third in the toilet roll by winding it around them so that they look like a mummy. If the toilet roll breaks, they must tuck the broken end in and carry on.

- Once done, players must then wind the paper back onto the toilet roll.

- The winning team is the one who completes the task first.

The Game of the Triffids

What's the game?

It's a bit like twister but requires more thought.

What do I need to play it?

At least five people for the game to be effective.

How many friends?

However many you can get your hands on. I'm sure there's a point when it stops being workable. Alternatively, you can split into teams to make it more competitive, but it is very funny if there are lots of you.

How do I play it?

- The format of the game is that teams compete to make a monster with varying numbers of limbs that touch the floor.
- To get started, you need to get everyone into teams of at least five. If you're playing in a small group then lose the team element and just get players to play in one group.
- The game leader then briefs the players that each team is to create a monster with a certain number of legs and arms touching the ground. If, for example, there are six players, the host might ask for a monster with nine legs and five arms.
- The teams then have to create this monster by putting the said number of limbs on the floor, while all still somehow remaining connected to each other.
- Start with a higher number of limbs to get the teams used to balancing, and then slowly decrease the number as they get better.
- Whoever's leading the game needs to have their wits about them and be able to do basic maths on the hoof.
- A point is awarded at the end of each round to the team that is quickest to form the monster with the correct number of limbs in contact with the ground while still remaining in contact with each other.

The Cornflake Heron

What's the game?

This game will appeal to yoga-ites as it allows guests to demonstrate their dexterity and balance. It's brilliant to watch and you might be surprised by the suppleness of some people in your group.

What do I need to play it?

An empty cereal carton.

How many friends?

As many as want to play it.

How do I play it?

- The aim of the game is to demonstrate flexibility by bending down and picking up a cereal packet using only the teeth as it gets lower and lower.
- Get everybody to stand in a circle and then each player takes it in turns to step forward, bend down and retrieve the cereal packet with their teeth. The rules are that no body part other than the player's feet are allowed to touch the floor, and no other object must give them balance.
- If players fail after two goes, they're out. If you want to be strict about it you can make it one go.
- Once the remaining players have completed the task you then need to trim the top layer off the cereal packet by about five centimetres. You then go around the circle again, with each player attempting to pick it up with their teeth within two goes.
- The game plays on, with the box getting lower and lower as more is ripped off at the end of each round, and more and more players dropping out, until the last man standing is declared the winner.

Cracker Whacker

What's the game?

Another kooky Victorian invention. This time you each tie six cream crackers to your head with a ribbon and then bash each other about the head with rolled-up newspapers until there's not a crumb left. I suppose those Victorians were fortunate enough to have maids and servants to clear up after them. Lucky them. We were left finding crumbs down the back of the sofa, in the drawers, under the bed, behind the toilet and so on, for months afterwards. Not for the fastidiously tidy.

What do I need to play it?

Six crackers each, a thick piece of ribbon and a rolled-up newspaper per player. You need to ensure your whackers are the same size per player to ensure that no one has an unfair advantage.

How many friends?

As many friends as you like. Bear in mind the maths when it comes to clearing up. You're going to be left with the remnants of cream-cracker crumbs of six multiplied by however many friends you have playing.

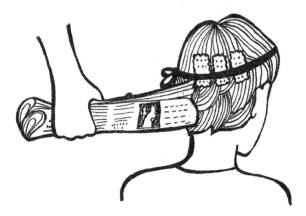

How do I play it?

- Distribute the cream crackers to ensure each player has six and then help each other out by tying them to your heads with a ribbon.

- You can tie them as a stack where you're happiest to get hit, e.g. on the back of your head, but you do run the risk of an unseen attack from behind. You need to be sure they're firmly held in place so they don't slip out. Alternatively, it's actually easier to tie a ribbon around your head and then slip the crackers in all around the ribbon. It's up to you which strategy you decide on.

- On the word 'Go!' players chase each other around the room with rolled-up newspapers and try to whack each other's crackers until they're all shattered away into crumbs.

- The last person with a decent cream cracker left tied to their head after all the bashing wins.

Musical Chairs

What's the game?

I've included Musical Chairs in this section as it works surprisingly well for adults. We've had many a party where the coolest kids in town have been found holding out until the bitter 'shoving your mate off the last chair' end. For those not familiar with the game, it involves dancing around chairs and dashing to sit down when the music stops.

What do I need to play it?

A stereo or something to make the music, and some chairs.

How many friends?

Brilliant for a huge group, but will obviously depend on how many chairs you've got.

How do I play it?

- First of all, line up two rows of chairs back-to-back down the middle of the room. You need a big playing space and to have cleared the other furniture out of the way. You also need to ensure that there are enough chairs minus one for everyone playing the game. If there are a few of you and it's after dinner, you can use your dinner table as the set-up. Just make sure you've properly cleared the table to prevent smashing of glasses or plates.

- Put the music on and get everyone to dance around the chairs. To make sure there's no aggressive chair-coveting, people need to keep moving around as they dance.

- At a point when people least expect it, turn the music off. Players must dash to a chair and sit down on it. The last person to do this is out. No lap-sitting is allowed.

- Before putting the music back on, move another chair out of the field of play, and game on.

- The game continues in the same format until there's one chair and two people. The first to sit down wins.

Improvisation

What's the game?

This is a game often played in drama schools as a warm-up.

What do I need to play it?

A wide and interesting selection of objects.

How many friends?

Ideally four or more.

How do I play it?

- Form teams of two. Each team is given an object to perform with in as many creative ways as possible – a Hula Hoop, for example. Hold it above your head and sing, 'Hark the herald angels sing'; hold it in front of you and say, 'You get a good view of the icebergs from this porthole'; or hold it as if driving a car and start yelling like Jeremy Clarkson.
- The winning team is the one with the most creative ideas.

Table Sock Wrestling

What's the game?

You'll need to ensure your guests aren't squeamish about fondling each other's feet, and you might want to have some clean socks on hand in case of any offensively dirty guests. This game involves battling to try to remove each other's socks.

What do I need to play it?

Some clean socks for each player. Make sure they're of the same elasticity and appropriate size for each wearer to prevent accusations of unfair advantage. The looser the socks are the better, otherwise matches can go on for quite a long time and get a little bit violent as time goes on.

How many friends?

However many pairs are up for playing it.

How do I play it?

- Depending on how much room and how many players you have to play, it's probably best to run this as a tournament with pairs competing and the winners making it through to the next rounds.
- Get your first playing pairs to face each other with their toes connecting. If you've got a lot of people then you might want to play multiple matches at the same time.
- On the word 'Go!' players must attempt to remove each other's socks using only their own feet.
- The first player to remove their opponent's socks wins.
- Winners then go on to play other winners until an ultimate champion is identified.

Dancing Game

What's the game?

This is a game that came out of fun-packed university years. It reached its peak when half a nightclub joined in, at a temple to Bristol hedonism known as Lakota. It used to have a fantastic balcony that overlooked the dance floor, where some friends and I managed to engage everyone in a session of mass organised fun. Since then, it's been rolled out on many an occasion and is brilliant to get reluctant dancers to join the floor. Persevere with this one and it'll be worth it.

What do I need to play it?

Some willing dancers.

How many friends?

You could play it with two of you, but definitely the more the better.

How do I play it?

- Get everyone to stand in a circle or at least in a position where you can all see each other.
- The first person starts and does a dance move – think John Travolta in *Saturday Night Fever*. The next person then leads the rest of the players to do the first move, before adding their own. To help people remember, it's useful to chant each move as it comes up.
- And so the game plays on until you've connected an entire routine that continues to grow and grow.

SEVEN

Classic Organised Fun for Kids

When compared to the children of today, those of yesteryear seem blessed with a magical time of freedom and discovery. Sunny days saw kids playing out on the street from dawn to dusk. Long bike rides led to discoveries of secret hideaways and dens, or ponds bubbling with frogspawn. Marbles and newspaper kites, tag and chalked-out hopscotch seem to recall a time of innocence and simple but captivating pursuits.

It's at kids' parties where many of these traditions have survived. For generations they have followed a much-loved formula. From the arrival of the children with their nervous smiles to the slice of cake wrapped in kitchen roll, there's a ritual to be adhered to. The same can also be said of the game-playing spectacle that ensues. It's a way for parents to relive their cherished childhood memories and pass them on for their children to share.

Nostalgia aside, the classics are also classics for a reason: they are simply brilliant games and their brilliance makes them as much fun for adults. Musical Chairs played at a New Year's Eve party is undeniably the best way to get things to move from a dull evening to a festival of feel-good anarchy.

The following chapter features a collection of those classic party games most of us cut our milk teeth on. Here are some warm reminders as well as some fresh inspiration to ensure your young friends will be thoroughly entertained.

Sardines

What's the game?

My uncle Ronald believes that Sardines was to blame for opening his eyes to the world of canoodling. He grew up at a time when mixed education was unheard of. This was long before the arrival of the six-inch rule (the maximum proximity allowed between boy and girl), introduced to prevent abandonment of morality when girls and boys started to go to school together.

Sardines, he soon learned, was an opportunity for permissible mixing of the sexes. With such intimate opportunities in mind it can also be lots of fun to play as adults. I can recall playing many post-pub games of this at our university halls of residence.

The game is a fun take on 'It', where children hunt out and join the person who's 'it' until all players end up stuffed in the cupboard or under the bed.

What do I need to play it?

Some good-sized hiding places.

How many kids and what age?

Unless you have the sort of endless cupboard found in *The Lion, the Witch and the Wardrobe*, this one's better played with small groups of say between three and six. Perfect for kids aged five and upwards.

How do I play it?

- Choose who's going to be 'it' first.
- The child runs off to hide while the others count to fifty.
- Depending on their age, you might need to help the hiding child to select a hiding place that's big enough to hold the number of children who are playing.
- Once the hiding child is safely hidden, the rest run to find him or her.
- As each child finds the hider, they join them in their hiding place until there is one child left doing the hunting, and it's then their turn to be 'it'.

Oranges and Lemons

What's the game?

The guest bedroom at my gran's house featured a pair of curtains decorated with chains of boys and girls skipping through orchards, some with their hands joined in arches and others dancing between trees laden with fruit. I spent hours lying in bed as a child staring at those curtains and itching to get up to play. As I never played the game as a child, it was only as an adult that I made the connection.

'Oranges and Lemons' is a nursery rhyme that dates back several centuries, and evolved into a popular childhood game. The rhyme sings of many of the churches of London, and its melody is said to match the sound of the different bells across the city.

The sinister end to the game involves chopping off the children's heads. It's believed children added this part of the rhyme some time in the late eighteenth century. The song refers to the execution of prisoners, many of whom were imprisoned for debt, hence the line, 'When will you pay me?'. The unfortunate prisoner would be informed of his impending death by a gallows man carrying a candle towards his cell ('Here comes a candle to light you to bed,') before the imminent end line: 'And here comes a chopper to chop off your head!'. A charming child's verse.

Although some might see it as a barbaric subject for a child's game, it's the infamous Roald Dahl-esque spirit that captures children's imaginations.

What do I need to play it?

Some willing children.

How many kids and what age?

You need at least six kids to make it work, though a roomful is much better. This one is great for kids over five.

How do I play it?

- To start, get your children into pairs and standing in a line. The first pair steps forward to form an arch by raising their hands up and clasping hold of their partner's hands in front of them.

- Players then file in pairs through the arch while everyone sings the words of the well-known nursery rhyme:

> 'Oranges and lemons,' say the bells of St Clement's,
> 'You owe me five farthings,' say the bells of St Martin's.
> 'When will you pay me?' say the bells of Old Bailey,
> 'When I grow rich,' say the bells of Shoreditch.
> 'When will that be?' say the bells of Stepney,
> 'I do not know,' says the great bell of Bow.
> Here comes a candle to light you to bed,
> And here comes a chopper to chop off your head!

- The challenge comes in the final three lines, and on the last word the children forming the arch drop their arms to catch the pair of children who are passing through at that point.

- When caught, these children are then out and must form another arch next to the existing one to create a steadily lengthening tunnel, through which the children to have to run faster and faster to escape.

- Some people also play it where the children chop down their arms all the way through the last line of the verse – it's up to you which variation you think works best.

Blind Man's Buff

What's the game?

Blind Man's Buff can be traced back to the Tudor period. There are some historical records showing it to be a popular with Henry VIII's courtiers, and its popularity was embedded further during those hearty Victorian parlour-game afternoons.

There's some confusion as to whether it's called Blind Man's 'Bluff' or 'Buff', but whether it's a naked or lying blind man, neither seems particularly politically correct. The British will generally choose the 'buff' variant, which is in fact nothing to do with nudity and is an old-fashioned word for a gentle push. The American's call it 'bluff', which might be as a result of poor transatlantic carriage or relate to the fact that 'bluff' is an old term for being blindfolded.

Call it what you choose, the game is yet another variant of It and remains a great way to entertain the kids as well as the adults on a rainy afternoon.

What do I need to play it?

A blindfold and an agreed space to play it.

How many kids and what age?

At least five of you to make it a decent game, and it works best with children aged seven and over.

How do I play it?

- Choose who's going to be 'it' first and put a blindfold on them.
- The rest of the players must then run away, but be contained within a confined space such as a garden or a room.
- The blindfolded player then has to try to catch the others who are running around and mocking them.

- Now, at this point there are three variants that you can choose to play:
  1. When a player is caught they're then out, and have to sit at the side.
  2. The caught person becomes the blindfolded player.
  3. Or the Victorians' favourite, where the blindfolded player has to guess who the caught person is by feeling their face and body – our stiff-upper-lipped relatives were quite racy really.

Musical Chairs

See Chapter Six: Organised Fun for Later in the Evening.

Musical Bumps

What's the game?

This is a great variation to Musical Statues, but this time involves the kids sitting down when the music stops. It's a good alternative when you're playing in large groups, as it's easier to spot the last child to sit down rather than the last one moving.

What do I need to play it?

A room or contained area, and some music. It might also be worth getting some arnica cream in for any overzealous bumping.

How many kids and what age?

Great for large groups aged five and over. I'd say you probably need a minimum of eight players to make it go on for any length of time.

How do I play it?

- Select your music and get your gang of kids to dance out on the floor in front of you.
- At any point in time, turn the music off and all the kids must quickly sit on the floor.
- Last one down is out and must go and sit quietly at the side. Last one left in is the winner.

Squeak Piggy Squeak

What's the game?

This is another parlour game favoured by those hyperactive young Victorians. It involves dizzily stumbling around and sitting on people's laps. It only really works if the kids know each other, to allow them to try to guess whose lap they're sitting on.

What do I need to play it?

A blindfold.

How many kids and what age?

You need at least six children aged five and upwards. This is another one that's great to play with large groups of kids.

How do I play it?

- Get your group to sit in a circle, blindfold whoever's going to go first and get them to stand in the middle.

- Someone then needs to turn the blindfolded child a good three times to make sure they're disorientated and dizzy.

- The child then has to scrabble around to find one of the children sitting in the circle. They sit on their lap and say 'Squeak piggy squeak', at which point the child whose lap the player is on lets out a squeak.

- The blindfolded player has to guess who it is. If they get it wrong, they have to carry on playing. If they get it right, it's the losing player's turn to be blindfolded.

Mulberry Bush

What's the game?

This game has rather sad beginnings. According to local history, the game originated in Wakefield Prison, where inmates used to exercise in the yard around a mulberry bush. Mothers who had their children alongside them in prison developed the game as a means of entertaining their charges. The bush still survives in the prison today, though I'm doubtful as to whether inmates hold up the tradition. It conjures a lovely image if they do.

What do I need to play it?

A gang of kids.

How many kids and what age?

You can play this with as large or small a group as you have to hand, and it's ideal for all ages.

How do I play it?

- Get everyone to stand in a circle and join hands, then skip around singing the following rhyme:

  Here we go round the mulberry bush,
  The mulberry bush, the mulberry bush.
  Here we go round the mulberry bush,
  On a cold and frosty morning.

- You then continue to sing another verse which substitutes going round the mulberry bush for another action that the children then act out. For example:

  This is how we mow the lawn,
  Mow the lawn, mow the lawn.
  This is how we mow the lawn,
  On a cold and frosty morning.

- And so the game plays on, with each of the children making up a different action for each verse. You can alternate the action verses by featuring the 'mulberry bush' verse in between.

Pass the Parcel

What's the game?

I can still remember the anticipation as we all watched the present move around the circle, wiling the music to stop when it passed through our sweaty fingers. The game was made even better when some enterprising parents placed sweet treats randomly between the wrapped sheets.

What do I need to play it?

A gift that has been wrapped up with lots of layers, and some flattish sweets such as lollipops to place between the sheets. Make sure there's a layer at least for each child. Also have some music to play while the parcel's being passed.

How many kids and what age?

It doesn't work very well with anything fewer than six children, but they can be of any age as long as there's an adult to lend a hand. Yet another one that's great for big groups and birthday parties.

How do I play it?

- Prepare your parcel by wrapping the prize in multiple layers and place flat sweets in between random sheets.
- Sit all the kids in a circle, put the music on and get them to pass the parcel around the circle.
- When the music stops, the child whose hands it is in takes off a layer of paper.
- Once completed, the music goes on again and the parcel is passed back around.
- The child who unwraps the last layer wins the prize.

Hopscotch

What's the game?

Hopscotch can be found dating back to the Roman Empire, when soldiers used the game to improve their footwork and agility in preparation for battle. The game continues to be played all over the world and has spawned many variants. I've featured the one most commonly found in school playgrounds today, along with some more novel variations for those looking to experiment.

What do I need to play it?

Some chalk, something to use as a marker and a pavement or tarmac to play on.

How many kids and what age?

Great to play on your own or in a small gang, and perfect for kids aged six and upwards.

How do I play it?

- To play this classic game, begin by chalking out your play area.

- The first player takes their marker (it can be a stone, or a coin, for example) and tosses it onto square number one.

- The hopper then has to hop up the course, missing the square that the marker landed on. They must be on one leg when it's a single square, or straddle both squares if it's a double.

- Once completed, they must then turn around and hop back, picking up their marker on the way, before throwing it onto the number two square and repeating the process.

- If the player falls over, misses a square or steps on the line, their go ends and it's the turn of the next player.

- Players always begin their turn where they last left off. The first player to complete the course working through the numbers wins the game.

Hunt the Slipper

What's the game?

This game dates back to 1766. There are many variations around the world, with the Americans playing a similar one called Huckle Buckle Beanstalk. In a nutshell, it's a simple game of Hide and Seek, with players hiding an object from a central player as they sit around them in a circle.

What do I need to play it?

A slipper or shoe.

How many kids and what age?

Six or more makes it a good game, and it's ideal for kids aged four and over.

How do I play it?

- Get the kids to sit in a circle and choose which one's going to be 'it'.
- Next, get the child who's 'it' to say the following to the group, before handing the shoe to one of the sitting children and going out of the room:

    Cobbler, cobbler, mend my shoe,
    Get it done by half past two.

- The child who's 'it' comes back into the room and has to guess who's got their slipper, as the sitting children surreptitiously pass the slipper between them.
- The game plays on until the child finally guesses correctly. If this is taking some time, you might want to offer them a helping hand. It's then their turn to be 'it'.

Classic Fun for Kids

Pin the Tail on the Donkey

What's the game?

Pin the Tail on the Donkey is one of our family's Christmas classics. We used to play innumerable variations, with Pin the Ear on Van Gough being a particularly memorable favourite, which for some reason my gran excelled at. It must have been her talented artistic leanings. There's a great alternative for teenagers called Pin the Kiss on the Poster that can be found in Chapter Nine: Organised Fun for a Few Kids.

What do I need to play it?

A blindfold and a picture of a donkey, ideally about one metre by half a metre in size. Draw and cut out a tail per player, and even get the kids to colour them in.

How many kids and what age?

This one's great to play in smaller groups, and works for children of a walking, talking age.

How do I play it?

- Hang your tailless donkey on the wall and hand out a tail to every player.
- Choose your first player, blindfold and spin them around to disorientate them, and if it is a young child, propel them gently in the general direction of the picture.
- The child then has to attempt to pin the tail on the donkey where they think it should go.
- The winner is the one who got closest to the appropriate tail-hanging place.

Stocking Balls

What's the game?

This was a real fad at school. I became rather good at it and can recall one occasion when three dinner ladies, the boy I fancied and the rest of the school stood watching my stocking-ball-bouncing brilliance. The game is believed to have originated around the Liverpool docks some time during the early twentieth century. The accompanying rhyme suggests that the playground craze at the time was more about smoking fags than collecting marbles. If you're happy to ignore this element, you'll have a thoroughly entertaining skill for your kids to master.

What do I need to play it?

A tennis ball and stocking per player, and a hard wall to bounce off.

How many kids and what age?

Great for kids to play on their own or in a small group. I'd recommend it for those aged six and upwards.

How do I play it?

- Put a ball in a stocking and get the child to stand with their back against the wall, holding the opposite end of the stocking to where the ball's hanging. They might want to wind it around their hand a couple of times to ensure it's secure.

- Now bounce the ball on the wall behind by swinging the stocking so that it bounces above right of the right shoulder, then swing it around so it bounces above left of the left shoulder. Finally swing it down so that it bounces between the legs before reversing back through this sequence.

- The elasticity of the stocking and the velocity of the movement will create a rhythmic feel that, once mastered, will have the child bouncing away for hours.

- Practise this until the three-bounce sequence can be done without thinking too much.

- Now practise doing a double bounce to either side.

Classic Fun for Kids

- Now practise alternating these movements. Once this can be done with ease, the child is ready to introduce the following rhyme:

  > Have a cigarette, Sir?
  > No, Sir.
  > Why, Sir?
  > Because I've got a cold, Sir.
  > Where did you get your cold, Sir?
  > At the North Pole, Sir.
  > What were you doing there, Sir?
  > Catching polar bears, Sir.
  > How many did you catch, Sir?
  > One, two, three, Sir.
  > The rest caught me, Sir.
  > Threw me in the sea, Sir.
  > That's the end of me, Sir.

- The child needs to bounce the ball using the three-bounce sequence all the way through until they get to the counting line 'One, two, three, Sir', where they do a double bounce before returning to the three-bounce sequence again.

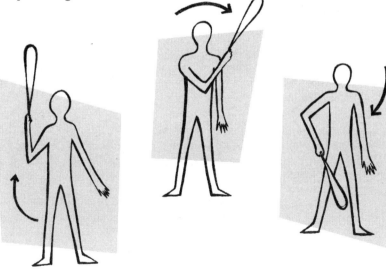

Dipping Rhymes

What's the game?

The ubiquitous game of 'It' is played by children across the world. It's one that every child seems to have a natural aptitude for. Dipping Rhymes are a fun way to help choose who's going to be 'it' by using them to count around a group of friends to see who's out at the end of each round. On the count of each word, the rhyme moves from one child to the next along a line or around a circle, the child where the rhyme ends being 'it'. The cigarette rhyme in Stocking Balls can be used in this way, and I've featured a couple of other examples below:

Ickle Ockle
Ickle ockle black bottle,
Ickle ockle out.
Ickle ockle ink bottle,
Out goes she.
Ickle ockle chockle bockle,
Ickle ockle out.
Ickle ockle chocolate bottle,
Ickle ockle out.

Each, Peach, Pear, Plum
Each, peach, pear, plum,
Out goes Tom Thumb;
Tom Thumb won't do,
Out goes Betty Blue;
Betty Blue won't go,
So out goes you.

Eeny, Meeny, Miney, Mo
Eeny, meeny, miney, mo,
Catch a tigger by the toe,
If he squeals let him go,
Eeny, meeny, miney, mo.

Eeny, meeny, miney, mo,
Sit the baby on the po,
When he's done
Wipe his bum,
Tell his mummy what he's done.

Chinese Counting
I went to a Chinese baker's shop
To buy a loaf of bread;
He wrapped it up in a ten-pound note
And this is what he said:
My name is . . .

Eany, meany, maca, raca,
Red rose, doma naca,
Ali Baba, suva naca,
Rum, tum, toosh.

Simon on the Railway
Simon on the railway,
Picking up stones;
Along came an engine,
And broke Simon's bones.
Oh, said Simon,
That's not fair.
Pooh, said the engine driver,
I don't care.

French Skipping

What's the game?

This was another playground top-ten game when I was young. My two best friends Leah and Adele and I played it endlessly, until it was banished from the playground when we caused a rather nasty tripping accident. I'm sure it's now banished from playgrounds across the country, so let's make sure it's not totally forgotten by encouraging kids to keep playing it.

What do I need to play it?

A two-and-a-half-metre-long piece of thick elastic with the two ends tied together to create a big loop.

How many kids and what age?

We picked it up when we were around seven or eight. You need a minimum of three kids to play it, or a few more if they don't mind a bit of waiting around.

How do I play it?

- Get two of the kids to face each other and step into the elastic with their ankles stretching it out, with the third child standing in the middle.
- The jumping child then starts with their left foot inside the elastic loop and right foot just outside, and then jumps over to the other side, so right foot is inside the loop and left foot is outside.
- You then repeat this sequence in time to a rhyme, with the last word featuring a new move, for example, both feet landing on the elastic:

  Chocolate cake, when you bake,
  How many minutes will you take?
  One, two, three, four.

  England, Ireland, Scotland, Wales,
  Inside, outside, inside, on!

Classic Fun for Kids

Old Mrs Mason broke her basin,
On the way to London Station.
How much did it cost?
One, two, three, four.

Charlie Chaplin sat on a pin,
How many inches did it go in?
One, two, three, four.

- The kids will need to play around with the rhymes and decide on an agreed sequence. If the player gets the routine wrong, they have to stop and swap to let another player have a turn.
- If they successfully get through the whole rhyme, the elastics are then raised to the knees, fondly known as 'kneesies', and then the thighs, 'thighsies'.

Musical Statues

What's the game?

This one's simple for children to grasp and only requires a stereo to play. Ideal to get the kids razzed up and excited, to kick off an afternoon of game playing.

What do I need to play it?

A stereo or something to make the music. You can strum or pluck a little ditty yourself, if you have the ability and inclination.

How many kids and what age?

At least eight to make it a decent game, and they need to be old enough to stand up, dance and stop. I'd say great for those aged four and over.

How do I play it?

- Get your gang to spread out in front of you and pop the music on.
- The children must then dance and lurch about in time to the music.
- You then turn the music off at intervals, at which point the kids must FREEZE.
- The last child (or children) to freeze is out and must sit on the floor at the side.
- If you've got a big group, keep one eye out for those cunning kids who slip around the sides and out of your view. The other often-played tactic is to move very slightly and slowly so that it's easier to stay stock still when commanded.
- The winner is of course the last child standing. The best bit about the game when I was a child were the adults who walked around you mid-freeze, tickling and pulling faces to try to make you laugh.

What's the Time, Mr Wolf?

What's the game?

This is a classic children's party game. It must have been Easter or some other day of religious celebration as I can recollect the tedium of Sunday school being replaced by an afternoon of games. I can still see the heavily patterned rug beneath my feet and hear the muffled ticking of the grandfather clock as we stepped towards our imminent deaths.

What do I need to play it?

Nothing at all.

How many kids and what age?

At least three, though it's great to play with a large group. Ideal for kids aged four and upwards.

How do I play it?

- Decide which child is going to be Mr Wolf and stand them facing the wall, with the other children in a line about three metres behind them.

- The children then all simultaneously say, 'What's the time, Mr Wolf?'

- The child who's Mr Wolf chooses a time and says, 'It's X o'clock'. The children then all step forward however many paces o'clock it is. The tension begins to ratchet up as the children get nearer to the wolf – especially if the wolf pretends to be very unconcerned . . .

- This goes on until Mr Wolf decides they've had enough and shouts, in reply to the question, 'It's dinner time!', and then turns around, chasing the squealing children until one is caught, whose turn it then is to become Mr Wolf.

EIGHT

Organised Fun for Lots of Kids

The thought of entertaining a heaving gaggle of kids will petrify most adults. That seething mass of boundless energy can be decidedly intimidating. But the truth of the matter is that organising fun is a piece of Bob the Builder cake as long as you follow four simple rules.

First, announce every game and activity with an abundance of enthusiasm and excitement. Children are likely to cheer with delight if you present each game as the most exciting thing they'll do since finding Rudolf had eaten the carrots left out for him on Christmas Eve. My sisters and I recently had the pleasure of organising the entertainment at our cousin Leon's fifth birthday party. The kids had whipped themselves into such a frenzy that we only had to bound along with the same air-punching delight and we'd have them squealing with glee at every suggestion.

The second golden rule is never show you're scared. Children have the same admirable power of perception as animals, and are able to sniff out a note of fear in a nanosecond. Delivery and conduct must ooze confidence at every step.

Thirdly, bribery works. From rewarding well-earned wins to encouraging game participation, a stash of chewy delights is the magic dust that will ensure proceedings go swimmingly. Sadly, not every child is blessed with a taste for pulses and greens, so you'll probably need something less wholesome than a carrot stick to guide them to your bidding.

Finally, ensure you have a plan bursting with game and entertainment ideas, and know what's coming next. The following chapter ensures you have an arsenal worthy of the Terminator, and is packed full of novel ideas to keep you in the driving seat at all times.

British Bulldog

What's the game?

I was never quite sure what the instigating factor was, but on occasion a rumour went around our school that everyone was going to play British Bulldog. The ripples of anticipation that went through each and every classroom was palpable and, by the time the bell rang for lunch, the entire school would come tumbling down the steps onto the tarmac and form themselves into one gargantuan heap that stood facing a single player.

The potential hairiness of this game always had the teachers hovering nervously on the periphery, muttering into fingers as to whether they should intervene. Keep an eye on any notoriously boisterous kids to ensure they don't get carried away in the excitement of it all.

What do I need to play it?

A big gang of kids and a large area to play in. It's also good to somehow mark out the play area with chalk if you're playing on tarmac. Alternatively, bags do the job just as well.

How many kids and what age?

Ideal for kids aged nine and upwards. You need at least eight kids to make it last a decent amount of time.

How do I play it?

- Mark out two lines behind which are the safety areas for players to race to.
- Choose who's going to be your 'bulldog' and position them in the middle, and get the rest of the kids to stand facing them at either end of the play area.
- When the bulldog shouts 'Go!' all the children charge towards him or her, and the bulldog has to 'tag' the other players.
- Once tagged, the caught player then joins the bulldog to try to catch the others.
- The same process plays out again, with the kids racing from opposite sides of the play area until there's one person left, who is then the winner.

Knights, Horses and Cavaliers

What's the game?

This is a wonderful alternative to Musical Statues and is on the money for kids who find the classics a little too childish.

What do I need to play it?

Nothing.

How many kids and what age?

Ideally an equal pairing of males and females in the group. Works best for kids aged eight and upwards. Also good for young teens, if you can tempt them out of their adolescent strop.

How do I play it?

- Get your young friends to pair up, ideally with someone from the opposite sex.
- When the music's on, the pairs must prance and dance around at will. When the music stops, the games facilitator shouts either 'Knight!', 'Horse!' or 'Cavalier!'
- 'Knight!' means the male has to give his partner a piggy back, 'Horse!' means the male has to give their partner a horse ride by getting on all fours and 'Cavalier!' means the male has to get down on one knee and the female sits on it.
- The last couple to execute the manoeuvre is out, and so the game plays on until the remaining couple is announced the winner.

Fun for Lots of Kids

Trawler, or Jack Fry

What's the game?

Trawler is a fun twist on the traditional game of Tag, where the kids who are 'had' join hands with each other and create a long trawling net to scoop up the remaining players.

What do I need to play it?

Some enthusiastic and energetic children, and an enclosed area to play in. A garden, field or the bit round by the bike sheds will do.

How many kids and what age?

This one's best played with at least six children, but definitely the more the better. The bigger the net, the easier it is to swing around and catch the others. Perfect for kids aged six to twelve, as it's very easy to pick up.

How do I play it?

- Agree who's going to be 'it'.
- The other players all run off in different directions within the agreed playing area and the child who's 'it' chases after them.
- When another child is caught, they join hands and proceed to chase the other children together.
- As more and more children join the line, they're able to start swinging around and capturing the remaining kids in their net.

Sack Race

What's the game?

The sack race used to be a fixture at country fairs, village fêtes and school sports days across the country, but as Britain moves towards an American-style litigation culture it's nuggets such as these that are starting to disappear. Make your protest heard by keeping the sack race alive before it falls victim to a fearsome health and safety culling.

The Sack Race is quite simply a race to the finish line, with your legs handicapped by being stuck in a sack. Traditionally, people used those old hessian potato sacks, but as they become harder to get hold of, you can conjure up a range of alternatives – see below. Contestants will try all sorts of techniques but, to master the art, the most effective is to make giant leaps with your feet close together.

What do I need to play it?

A sack per racer. If the kids are small enough, you can use pillowcases.

How many kids and what age?

As many as you can fit on your racecourse, and someone to act as umpire. Ideal for kids aged eight and upwards.

How do I play it?

- Get the youngsters in their sacks lined up at the start of the course.
- On the word 'Go!' racers need to bounce their way down the designated course, racing to be the first across the finishing line.

Fun for Lots of Kids

Balloon Race

What's the game?

Children find these giddy antics as much fun as their adult counterparts, and the images the game delivers will certainly add colour to your summer photo album.

What do I need to play it?

A balloon per racer.

How many kids and what age?

As many as will fit on the start line. Great for kids aged seven and upwards.

How do I play it?

- Get the kids lined up at the starting line, each with a balloon in hand.
- On the word 'Go!' the children race to the finishing line, batting their balloon in front of them.
- If the balloon touches the floor or the child holds rather than bats it, then they have to go back to the starting line. First across wins.

Traffic Control

What's the game?

This game takes a bit of explaining, but it's worth the invested time. It involves the kids spinning around in circles and trying not to be the one left without a partner. It's great to play with a large group of kids and has them giggling and giddy within minutes.

What do I need to play it?

Nothing at all.

How many kids and what age?

The more kids, the more fun you'll have. You'll also need an adult to be 'traffic controller'. This one's suitable for kids aged between six and ten.

How do I play it?

- Get the kids to split into two groups, with one having one more child in than the other.

- Get the smaller group to link hands and form a circle, and then ask the larger group to do the same by forming another circle around them.

- The traffic controller needs to explain the rules of the game: 'Green!' means they start spinning in opposite directions, 'Red!' they stop and 'Brakes!' means the inner circle only sit on the ground.

- On the word 'Green!' the two circles start to go round in opposite directions. When the traffic controller shouts 'Red!' the children stop and reach out to hold hands with the person that is in front of or behind them.

- The child in the outer circle who is left without someone to hold hands with is then out.

Fun for Lots of Kids

- Next it's the inner circle's turn. Start the circles spinning again and when you shout 'Brakes!' the inner circle must sit on the ground. The last person to sit down is also out.
- The circles then start spinning in opposite directions again, and the game continues until there is one child left in the middle, who is then the winner.

Circle Ball

What's the game?

This game's broadly based on the American game Dodgeball, which for some reason has never taken off in the UK.

What do I need to play it?

A ball, preferably quite soft.

How many kids and what age?

You really need sixteen or more kids to make it work. This one's great for children aged between eight and twelve.

How do I play it?

- Get your gang to split into two teams.
- One team forms a circle, with the others standing inside it.
- The aim of the game is for the children on the outer circle to 'touch' the children who are running around inside the circle by throwing the ball.
- As soon as the child is 'had', they then join the outer circle.
- The rules are that for a score to be counted, the ball must be thrown non-aggressively and must not hit the child on the head.
- Last child left in the middle is the winner, and then the teams swap.

Tangle

What's the game?

This is very funny to watch. The likelihood of the kids managing to undo themselves is very low, but it's brilliant to see them trying to figure out how.

What do I need to play it?

Nothing.

How many kids and what age?

The more the merrier. Suitable for kids aged six to ten.

How do I play it?

- Get your group to stand in a circle facing each other and close their eyes. They now need to walk towards each other with their arms held out, ensuring their eyes are firmly shut, and grab whoever's hands they come across.

- When all linked up, the children must open their eyes and try to figure out how they can untangle themselves without letting go of each other's hands.

Fun for Lots of Kids

Fancy-Dress Pass the Parcel

What's the game?

Same rules as for Pass the Parcel, but for this one, every time the music stops the player holding the parcel has to take an item of clothing out of a bag and put it on.

What do I need to play it?

Get a sack or lightweight bag and fill it full of lots of different items of clothing – the funnier the better. Think stupid wigs, or kids dressed in adults' clothes, and you get the idea. You'll also need a stereo to play some music to accompany the passing.

How many kids and what age?

Great for large groups of children aged five and upwards.

How do I play it?

- Collect your dressing-up clothes together and put them in the bag.
- Next, get all the children to sit in a circle.
- When the music starts, the children have to pass the bundle around, and when the music stops they have to reach in, pull out an item and put it on.
- The music then starts again and the game continues.
- The child who puts the last item on is the winner.

Duck, Duck, Goose

What's the game?

I remember playing this in my school playground. It's one of those games that is easy for kids to pick up and pass on to their friends.

What do I need to play it?

Some willing children.

How many kids and what age?

At least six to make it a decent game. Good for kids aged six and upwards.

How do I play it?

- Get the kids to form a circle with one child nominated as 'it'.
- When ready to go, whoever is 'it' has to go around the circle tapping the other children on the head in turn, saying 'Duck, duck, duck'. At any random point the child will tap one of the other sitting children on the head and say 'Goose', and then pelt around the circle.
- The selected child has to jump up immediately and pelt around the circle in the opposite direction.
- The last person back to the missing space is then 'it', and so the game goes on.

Fun for Lots of Kids

Sleeping Lions

What's the game?

It took me some time to figure out why Sleeping Lions was always the last game on any birthday party agenda, but I was never the smartest kid on the block. For those who don't know it, it's the perfect way to pacify a gaggle of razzed-up, sugar-fuelled kids.

What do I need to play it?

Some children who need to calm down.

How many kids and what age?

As many or as few as you have, of any age.

How do I play it?

- Explain to the children that you're going to play a game of Sleeping Lions and that it involves lying on the floor and being as quiet and as still as is possible.
- If a child moves, they are out, and they have to sit quietly at the side of the room.
- If it's been a particularly energetic day, you might be lucky enough to have a few children who drift gently off to sleep.

Clappers

What's the game?

This is a vital tool that teachers use to instil control in a classroom, eliciting the opening bars of rebellious cries. It's ideal to get kids to stop and tune in to you, rather than joining Johnny in a game of who can shriek the loudest. It captures the little tykes' attention and gets them to sit stock still, ears pricked and back on their best behaviour.

What do I need to play it?

Some good clapping hands.

How many kids and what age?

As many as there are in the room. It's particularly good for large groups of young kids aged four and upwards.

How do I play it?

- This game involves the children mimicking the leader's clapping sequences, and listening out and being quiet when they hear the sequence they shouldn't follow.
- First of all, you need to decide on a 'leader only' clapping sequence that the children shouldn't follow. It might be five fast claps, or three slow and two quick, for example. The leader identifies a rhythm at the beginning and makes sure all the children are aware of it.
- The leader then claps out a variety of short sequences. After each one, the children clap it out themselves. If the leader claps the 'leader only' sequence, then anyone who claps after this one is out.
- Try to make sure there aren't any very young or slower kids in the group as they may feel penalised for not getting the game as quickly as the others.

Fun for Lots of Kids

Balloon Volleyball

What's the game?

This is a gentler variation of Beach Volleyball. It has the added advantage of preventing windows getting smashed or tears erupting when a ball is smacked in someone's face.

What do I need to play it?

A balloon and something for a makeshift net, for example a rope strung across your garden.

How many kids and what age?

Enough to make two teams, and they need to be old enough to grasp the rules. I'd suggest this one's suitable for children over eight.

How do I play it?

- String up your net and get the kids set up in their two teams either side of the net.
- Give the first team the balloon and explain to them that they have to hit it over the net to the other team. The other team must then hit it back. If a team doesn't manage to hit it back, or allows the balloon to hit the floor, the opposing team gets one point.
- You can introduce additional volleyball rules once the kids get the idea, but by the time they grasp the basics with a balloon you could always promote them to start playing the real game.
- The team with the highest score at the end of the set period wins.

Jaws

What's the game?

I imagine most children, particularly in this day and age, are fairly clueless as to who Jaws is. Much to my playground shame, I wasn't even allowed to watch the film when I was a child. This game involves splitting your group into shark and fish, who then chase each other around the harbour walls. Be prepared for a screaming mass of kids.

What do I need to play it?

A pile of clothes or bags to mark out the harbour walls.

How many kids and what age?

At least twelve kids aged seven and over.

How do I play it?

- First of all, set up your harbour walls by laying out the bags and coats in a long (five-metre) line, leaving an opening of about two metres marking the harbour entrance.
- Get the kids to stand in a line and give each the name of a different type of fish – plaice, cod, mackerel, for example – and then the fourth person is the shark. It might be worth running through their names a couple of times to make sure they know who they are.
- Once established, you need to manoeuvre everyone to get all the fish on one side of the wall and the sharks on the other.
- Now shout out the different fish names in turn, and as each name is called the fish leave the harbour. Once they're all out, encourage them to swim about and around each other.
- When they're least expecting it, you shout 'Shark attack!' and the sharks leap over the wall and into action to try to catch a fish. Meanwhile, the fish must try to run back into the harbour through the harbour entrance. Once in the harbour entrance, the fish are then safe.
- Any fish caught by the sharks are out and must go and sit at the side.
- The game plays on until there's only one fish left, who's the winner.

Stepping Stones

What's the game?

This is a race across the room but players are only allowed to step on pieces of newspaper that they lay out in front of them.

What do I need to play it?

Two sheets of newspaper per player.

How many kids and what age?

A good crowd to make it a race. It really depends on the room you have available to play the game. This one's suitable for children aged six upwards.

How do I play it?

- Get the kids to line up at a designated starting point with their sheets of paper in hand.
- On the word 'Go!' they have to race to the finish line, but are only allowed to tread on the sheets of paper that they laid out in front of them. As they step with both feet onto the first sheet they need to lay out their second sheet, and so they move forwards, turning around to pick up the sheet behind them to bring it to the front for them to step on, and so on.
- To introduce an element of pretend danger, you could make it clear that the carpet is shark-infested – make sure you stick to the stepping stones!
- The first to the finish line wins.

Opposites

What's the game?

This game plays to kids' natural desire to be naughty. It gives them permission to do the total opposite to what you're asking. It's not one for the very young as it requires an element of thinking ahead.

What do I need to play it?

Enough room to play in.

How many kids and what age?

This one's suitable for children aged six and upwards, and you need at least eight of them to make it a decent game.

How do I play it?

- The aim of the game is for the children to do exactly the opposite of what you're asking them to do. If you were to say 'Walk,' then they should run; if you were to say 'Wave with your right hand,' then they should do so with their left. You just need to be careful that there is a clear opposite to what you're asking them to do.
- If the children get it wrong, they're out.
- Last kid standing is the winner.

Shoe Tag

What's the game?

Another variation on the classic game of Tag. This one gives the kids two lives and has the added attraction of having their shoe stuffed down their trousers or skirts to keep them absorbed that little bit longer.

What do I need to play it?

Children with shoes that fit down the back of their trousers or skirts. If the girls are wearing dresses then you'll need something that can be used to make belts.

How many kids and what age?

A big, rambling crowd of kids aged six and above.

How do I play it?

- Get the kids to put their shoes either down the backs of their trousers or skirts or tucked securely underneath a belt. You need to ensure that each child has a reasonable amount of shoe sticking out of the top so that the other kids can grab it.
- Choose who's 'it', and whoever it is has to chase after the kids and try to pull a shoe out of the backs of their trousers, skirt or belt.
- Once a shoe is grabbed it is put at the side. When both a player's shoes are taken, they are then 'it'.

Corners

What's the game?

This game's a great one to start off the party entertainment. It's easy to explain and quick for the kids to grasp.

What do I need to play it?

A room with four corners.

How many kids and what age?

Lots and lots. The more the better, as ten is the minimum that you can really play with. Children need to be seven and above to fully get the idea.

How do I play it?

- Choose a room with four corners and number them one to four, making sure all the kids know which corner is which number.
- Choose which child is going to be 'it' first, and blindfold them.
- The rest of the children then split up randomly and run to one of the four corners of the room.
- The blindfolded child then shouts out a number and all the children in that corner are out.
- The kids then break up again and run to another corner in the room, and so the game plays on until there's one child left, whose turn it is to be blindfolded next.

Over and Under

What's the game?

This is a simple relay race involving passing the balloon over the children's heads and between their legs.

What do I need to play it?

Two balloons.

How many kids and what age?

Ideally you need at least eight children to make two teams of four. This one works for kids aged six and over.

How do I play it?

- Get your gang to split into two teams and form two straight lines in front of you.
- Give each child at the front of the line a balloon.
- On the word 'Go!' the children have to alternately pass the balloon over their heads and between their legs.
- When it gets to the last person, they have to run to the front and do the same all over again, until the person who started is back at the front.
- Whichever team completes the task first wins.

Fun for Lots of Kids

Islands

What's the game?

This is a great alternative to Musical Chairs if you don't have enough chairs to play with. The same rules apply but you just use newspapers instead.

What do I need to play it?

An old newspaper and some music

How many kids and what age?

A minimum of six to make it a decent length game. This one's ideal for kids aged five and over.

How do I play it?

- Ensure you've got enough room to play in relation to the number of children.

- Lay out sheets of newspaper at a reasonable distance apart from each other to create 'islands' on the floor, or grass. Make sure there's one sheet less than the number of children playing.

- Play the music and get the children to skip and dance around the sheets. When the music stops, the children have to leap onto the sheets and the child with no sheet to stand on is out.

- You then remove one of the sheets as each child is out, until you have the last child playing, who is then declared the winner.

NINE

Organised Fun for a Few Kids

One of the joys of hanging out with kids is the freedom of their imaginations. They have that enviable ability to transport themselves to another world that can absorb and cocoon them for hours.

Some of the childhood games my siblings and I enjoyed the most were the ones we invented ourselves. There's a tree called Sundowner that lives by the river at the bottom of my aunt's garden, whose place in family history is secured. If you squint at the tree at dusk, her statuesque figure and flat bottom trunk means she can look a little bit like a horse. Together Sundowner and I won many Grand Nationals, but we soon decided to escape the cruelty of fame by running away in a gypsy caravan with my sisters in tow. These elaborate tales entertained us for weeks over long, lazy Devonshire summers, and afforded my mum and aunt sacred time to float down the river in a rubber dinghy sipping their G&Ts.

Often, children need a helping hand to guide them on their game-playing way. My aunt Mary Rose was always a sure bet to come up with a new and cunning idea that would entertain us for most of the day. She had a wonderful ability to customise a croquet set from an eclectic collection of household paraphernalia, or plant an idea of where and how to build a new and magical den that would have us squirrelling away for hours.

Fun for a Few Kids

Such experiences become magical childhood memories when they're relived and shared with generations of family and friends. The following chapter features a selection of game ideas that are designed to be adapted and evolved at will. I hope there's something here to inspire family traditions and pave the way to create some treasured memories of your children's own.

Helicopter Ride

What's the game?

This game belongs to my boyfriend's dad. It's a much anticipated feature of the Girling family Christmas and has the kids scrabbling for their turn every year. It involves taking the child on a helicopter ride and provides the exhilarating feeling of lifting high into the air when they're actually only half a metre off the ground.

One of the now-famous Brit artists did something similar several years ago by offering helicopter rides at an art event. It involved them standing a gallery visitor in front of their sculpture of a miniature landscape, grabbing them around the waist, lifting them a few centimetres off the ground and screaming, 'Look at the little cows and sheep and hedgerows in the field below!'

What do I need to play it?

A chair, a book and a blindfold.

How many kids and what age?

You need four people in total. One player (the child) and ideally three adults to help out. This one will appeal to children aged four and over.

How do I play it?

- Blindfold the first passenger and stand them on a chair.
- Two of you then stand either side of the chair and the passenger places their hands on the heads of the two lifters to steady themselves.
- A commentary is then provided as the helicopter 'takes off' and travels high up into the clouds.
- As the commentary is given, the two people either side of the chair lift it about ten centimetres off the ground while simultaneously bending their knees and lowering their heads. This does take a small degree of strength.
- By doing this, the child is given the exhilarating feeling that they're lifting off high into the sky. The commentary continues: '. . . You are now

flying over the green hills. There's a farmyard below with some cows and sheep in the fields. We're now going to travel much higher . . .'.

- As you say this, someone steps behind the child and slowly lowers a large hardback book on their head to give the feeling that they've hit the ceiling. At this point the child can take their blindfold off and they'll be mightily surprised that they're actually so close to the ground.
- The other way you can do it is to ask the child to jump off the chair before removing the blindfold. There have been a few tears with this route, however, so maybe stick to the book option.

Nice and Clean Ice Cream

What's the game?

Not one if you're particularly house-proud. If you are, I'd suggest you get the kids to play it outside. It's essentially a competition to see who's best at feeding their opponent while wearing a blindfold.

What do I need to play it?

Two blindfolds and two bowls of ice cream, with spoons.

How many kids and what age?

Two to play and lots to watch and laugh. Ideal for kids aged eight and over.

How do I play it?

- Blindfold the two playing children and sit them facing each other.
- Put the bowl of ice cream in front of them and give them each a spoon.
- On the word 'Go!' the children must try to feed each other. Whichever child manages to feed their opponent with the least amount of mess wins.

Admiral Nelson

What's the game?

Whenever I recall playing this game a clear memory comes to mind of me in my favourite floral floor-length orange nylon party number, in a chintzy 1980s living room, with leftover vol-au-vents and cheese-and-pineapple sticks on the table behind.

Whether it was invented in the 1980s or not, this game engaged a generation of children and deserves to be rolled out for many more to come.

What do I need to play it?

A hat, a coat, a blindfold and anything else that might represent something you'd find onboard a ship. You also need to prepare some egg cups full of jelly that have been set in the fridge. Ideally one per child.

How many kids and what age?

As many or as few as you have, and ideal for children aged six and over.

Fun for a Few Kids

How do I play it?

- First of all, you need to prepare your ship. You need to figure out how you can convert your house or flat into a seafaring galleon. Perhaps it's your kitchen that becomes the ship's galley, with someone on hand sharpening knives, or the patio that becomes the deck, with someone making the noise of the gulls. Use your imagination and plan your route around the boat, ideally with props on hand.

- Before you start playing, it's worth attempting to give the children a history lesson so that, in the broadest terms, they know who Admiral Nelson is. If possible, show them a picture of him in his hat.

- Next, you need to shepherd the children out of the room and get them to wait outside the door until they're called in.

- As their turn comes up, a blindfold is put on them and they're led into the room one at a time.

- As each child comes into the room, you tell them you've managed to get hold of Admiral Nelson's body. First of all, you pass them the hat and say, 'This is Admiral Nelson's hat.' You then pass them the coat and say, 'This is Admiral Nelson's coat.'

- Finally, you ask the child to stick their forefinger out and you say, 'This is Admiral Nelson's eye,' as you poke the child's finger in the egg cup of jelly.

- It's advised that you quickly remove the blindfold to prevent them getting upset.

Submarine

What's the game?

This one's best played with kids who don't know the game. Rather surprisingly, however, those who have played before still love to put themselves through the water-drenching turmoil yet again. This game is about taking a passenger on a submarine ride and the perils of a leaky periscope.

What do I need to play it?

An anorak and a glass of water.

How many kids and what age?

One's enough, but any more can be just as fun. I'd suggest playing it with children aged seven and over to prevent too many tears.

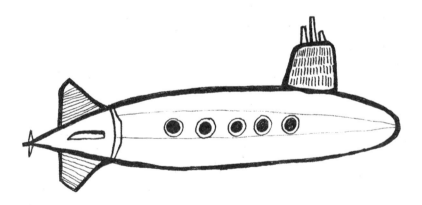

How do I play it?

- First of all, you need to find a willing passenger who fancies a day trip on a submarine.

- Once nominated, zip them into the anorak without their arms in the sleeves, so that the arm of the coat extends upwards from the face. Get them to lie on the floor while you pull the coat arm up, and then ask them to peer up through the coat arm as though it is a periscope.

- Next, you need to set them to sail on their adventure by talking them through what's happening:

  'OK, Captain, are you ready to set sail? Good. OK, we're leaving port now, Sir. We'll be sailing out through to the middle of the bay with half the submarine raised above water. OK, we need to start submerging, the first part of the submarine is under. The main bridge and top of the submarine are now also under, but the periscope is still out. We're going to now fully submerge and bring the periscope in. Are you ready, Sir?'

- When the child answers 'Yes' you say 'OK, we're diving down', and then tip the glass of water down the periscope straight into the child's face, to what will hopefully be squeals of delight.

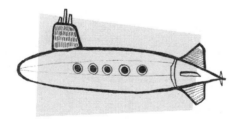

Fishing

What's the game?

This one's great for having in the cupboard ready to roll out when you've got a handful of grizzling kids stuck inside out of the rain. It takes a little preparation but that is half the fun.

What do I need to play it?

To do a proper job on this, you really need to make a trip to your local DIY store. Alternatively, you can fashion most of these elements using the contents of your recycling bin:

- Wooden dowelling (although a few strong twigs should suffice).
- Some string.
- Those screw-in hooks.
- Small offcuts of wood.
- Acrylic paint and other waterproof bits and pieces for decoration.
- Something to make your pond; a washing-up bowl is ideal.

How many kids and what age?

However many you have to entertain, and it works for children aged five and over.

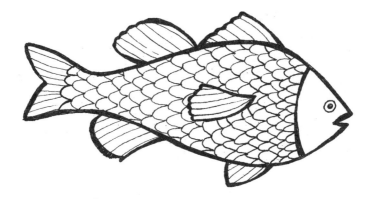

How do I play it?

- First of all, you need to create your fishing rods. Take your twig or wooden dowelling, cut to about 50 centimetres long and securely attach a piece of string with a loop tied in one end.

- Next, you need to fashion your fish using your offcuts of wood. You can be as creative as you like with this; definitely have a rumble in your recycling bin for decorative bits. We cut up a pile of those shiny crisp wrappers and looped and taped them to form elaborate fins and tails. The only thing you need to ensure is that you attach a large hook to its top side. Once rod and fish are ready, simply set them afloat in your pond and start fishing. You can assign different points to different fish to add a competitive element to the game.

- I'd also suggest letting the children take it in turns rather than having a free-for-all. It'll only end up in tears and tangled rods.

The Silhouette Game

What's the game?

This is actually a Victorian parlour game that will have the kids in stitches. I've played this many a time with adults, though it's fairly easy to guess who's who, and it's the silhouetted performance that provides the most entertainment. If you are playing it with adults, it's great to use as the entrance piece to the dinner party before everyone knows who's there. That way people have to guess who's behind the sheet as each guest arrives.

What do I need to play it?

A strong torch and a sheet, and something to suspend the sheet from. This is one to play in a darkened room as you need the lack of light to create the silhouettes with torches. You'll also need two adults to hold the sheet if there's nothing else to suspend it from, one adult to hold the torch and another to run the guessing game on the other side.

How many kids and what age?

You need at least six of them to make the guessing part work. This one works best with children aged seven and over.

How do I play it?

- First of all, you need to set up your room by finding somewhere to hang your sheet so that it's suspended like a curtain all the way down to the floor (this is crucial to prevent any shoes giving the game away). If you can't find anything to do this, then you'll need two adults to stand on chairs and hold the sheet up so that it hangs down to the floor.
- Divide the children into two teams.
- Next, you need to test your apparatus to ensure that you can get your room dark enough and that your torch is strong enough to create a silhouette.
- Once set up and ready to go, get the children to split into two teams. The first team goes out of the room, to a spot from which they can easily access the back of the sheet, while the others stay in the room.

- The team from outside the room then take it in turns to go behind the sheet with the torch shining behind them to create their silhouette. They must then silently dance or create funny shapes while the children from the other team try to guess who it is.
- They get three guesses and, if guessed correctly, the child then reveals themselves.
- The game plays on until all children are identified and the teams then swap places.

How Small Can You Write Your Name?

What's the game?

As ridiculous as this game sounds, it entertained my friend and his grandfather for hours. They used to sit at the table, testing each other's writing accuracy and eyesight as they delicately etched out their names using the smallest letters possible. The game quite simply is exactly what it says on the tin.

What do I need to play it?

A pen and paper.

How many kids and what age?

As many or as few as you like, and they need to be old enough to write.

How do I play it?

See who can write their name the smallest.

Trussed-Up Turkeys

What's the game?

This is very amusing to watch. You need to ensure the kids are careful not to bash each other too much, as it's one where they can get easily carried away.

What do I need to play it?

Two ropes or scarves, and two walking sticks, broomsticks or umbrellas.

How many kids and what age?

You need two to battle and the rest to watch. I'd suggest playing it with children aged seven and over.

How do I play it?

- First of all, choose which children are going to play and then prepare them for their duel.
- With the children sitting on the floor, you need to tie each child's ankles together, position the stick or umbrella under their knees and get them to pull their knees bent up to their chests.
- Next, get them to hook their elbows under the umbrella and clasp their hands, still with elbow bent, up in front of them as if in prayer.
- When securely positioned, move each child so that they're facing each other with toes touching.
- On the word 'Go!' the children battle to try to knock the other over by using their feet to flip the other child off balance. Keep an eye as well to make sure the ends of the sticks don't jab the other child.
- The rules are that knees and elbows must remain bent to ensure the child maintains their trussed-up position.
- A tournament format can be created where simultaneous games are played, ending in a final trussed-turkey battle.

Fun for a Few Kids

Waterslide

What's the game?

When I was a child, summers used to be as summers should be: full of sunshine and blissfully hot. I can remember endless after-school hours or balmy weekends playing on our waterslide. It was ideal for preventing a gathering of crotchety and hot kids.

What do I need to play it?

An area of long grass – ideally on a slope – a hose attached to a tap, and some long strips of plastic.

How many kids and what age?

However many are around to play. Great for kids of all ages.

How do I play it?

Lay out your plastic on the grass and turn the hose on so that it runs down one end. Kids then charge towards the plastic and skid along it, soaking and squealing along the way.

Bicycle Obstacle Course

What's the game?

An advanced lesson in cycling, teaching balance, focus and courage by getting your young friends to cycle their way around a designated course.

What do I need to play it?

A child's bike and whatever you have to hand to create an obstacle course.

How many kids and what age?

As many as would like to play. They need to be of bike-riding age, and have mastered the art without stabilisers.

How do I play it?

- First up, you need to create your course using objects that are around your house or garden. Think about flowerpots the kids could weave in and out of, a bridge made from a plank across your garden pond (if you're feeling brave), a basket hung from a tree that they need to grab as they cycle past, or a challenging track to cycle over made from an old duvet laid on the grass. The ideas are endless. Your best bet is to have a dig around the paraphernalia in your garden shed or attic.
- Once set up, challenge each child to cycle around the course, completing allocated tasks on the way.

Ringing Hide and Seek

What's the game?

This one's a modern twist on Hide and Seek where clues are fed by mobile phone calls.

What do I need to play it?

Two mobile phones.

How many kids and what age?

A minimum of three kids aged seven and upwards.

How do I play it?

- Whoever's hiding first takes the mobile phone while the others count to sixty before shouting, 'Coming, ready or not!'

- The children proceed to hunt around the house to try to find the hidden person. If they can't find them after sixty seconds they can call the mobile phone and the hider must give one clue.

- While one child is making the call, the other child needs to run around the house listening to the ringing of the mobile phone, as this is also a key clue as to where the child is hidden.

- A maximum of three clues can be given, by which time if the hider is still not to be found then they're declared the winner.

Banker Broker

What's the game?

This is a game that used to be played by kids living in Brooklyn, New York. It's a brilliant lesson in the basics of banking and teaches kids the principles of playing the market.

What do I need to play it?

A bowl and some nuts if you want to follow the traditional rules, but coppers, marbles or even stones work just as well.

How many kids and what age?

A good three or four, and they need to be old enough to have a basic grasp of maths.

How do I play it?

- Choose who's going to be banker, leaving the rest of the players to be depositors.
- The banker places the bowl on the ground and draws a line half a metre or so away.
- Depositors pay the banker one nut to play, and then throw a handful of nuts simultaneously to try to get them into the bowl.
- If an even number of items land in the bowl, the banker pays out, returning the nuts that landed in the bowl and matching them from the bank. If an odd number lands in the bowl, the depositor loses them all.
- If a depositor manages to get all of their nuts in the bowl, they become the banker.

Malteser Game

What's the game?

This was a feature at my childhood birthday parties. It involves sucking a Malteser onto the end of a straw and racing to see who gets the most into their pot.

What do I need to play it?

A large bag of Maltesers, a bowl and a timer. Then a straw and a glass or cup per player.

How many kids and what age?

However many are around; it works best for children aged eight and over.

How do I play it?

- Empty your Maltesers into the bowl and place it in the middle of the table. Each player sits around it with a straw and cup in hand.
- Children take it in turns to have thirty seconds to use the straw to suck and transport the Maltesers from the bowl in the middle to the cup in their hand.
- Once everyone's had their go, the child with the most Maltesers in their cup wins.

Pin the Kiss on the Poster

What's the game?

I've included this game in the kids' chapter, but it's great fun for adults as well. There's a particular pleasure that can be derived from watching your puckered and rouged uncle stagger towards a picture of his favourite politician and attempt to plant a kiss on his lips.

What do I need to play it?

Some full-fat Marilyn Monroe red lipstick, and a poster or picture from a magazine of your selected idol or figure of dislike.

How many kids and what age?

Any more than six and the game loses its momentum. Smaller groups are much better. This one's great for the younger kids as it's easy for them to grasp. It works for anyone aged four and upwards.

How do I play it?

- First of all, hang the picture of your idol at kissing height for the players.
- Next, children take it in turns to put the blindfold on and layer up with a good coating of lipstick.
- When ready, the child is spun around several times to achieve disorientation and is then gently propelled towards the poster.
- The object of the game is for the child to attempt to kiss the idol's lips. Every time a kiss is planted, you write the child's name near it so you know whose kiss it is.
- The closest wins.

Stalkers

What's the game?

This is another game that seems synonymous with children's parties in the 1980s. I remember playing it at Girl Guides before I got asked to leave for bad behaviour. The esteemed thinking was that it taught us to listen and respond to our senses.

What do I need to play it?

A chair, a blindfold and a set of keys.

How many kids and what age?

A minimum of three to make it fun, and works best with kids aged seven and over.

How do I play it?

- Decide which child is going first and pop the blindfold on them, before sitting them on the chair with the set of keys underneath it.
- When ready, the other children have to try and sneak up one by one, without being 'sensed', and snatch the keys from under the chair where the child is sitting.
- The child on the chair has to sense where they are by pointing in the direction they think the stalking child is coming from.
- If they get it right, the child who was busted becomes the 'stalked'.

Murder in the Dark

What's the game?

This is a macabre classic that I know has multiple variations. I've featured the one we used to play when we were children as I think it's fairly close to the original form. We used to love this game as it allowed us to scream and gurgle in agony as we writhed and wriggled to our gruesome deaths.

The game involves everyone drawing a card out of a hat to find out if they're the 'murderer', 'victim' or 'detective' and then running around in the dark acting out their roles. If you don't have any cards to hand you could write the roles on slips of paper. My brother once tricked us all by secretly doctoring the papers so that everyone was the murderer. The sound that emitted from our house that night was akin to an evening in a Victorian prison.

What do I need to play it?

A hat, a pack of cards and a very dark room.

How many kids and what age?

You need a minimum of four to play, aged eight and over.

How do I play it?

- First of all, sort through a deck of cards and pull out an ace, a jack, a king, a queen and number cards for the amount of remaining players.
- Next, get all the players to discreetly choose a card from the pack. All the cards have a meaning and you need to let the players know who they are while making sure they don't tell anyone else: ace is the murderer, the jack is the detective, the king is the detective if the jack dies and then the queen is the detective if the jack and the king both die. The number cards are other potential victims.
- Once everyone knows who they are, collect the cards and put them to the side for the next game.
- Next, turn off all the lights so that it's completely dark and get everyone to spread out through the house as quietly as possible. You may need to

encourage some of the kids to leave their friends as it's important that everyone disappears on their own.

- And this is where the anarchy begins to take shape. Victims are trying to avoid the murderer, the murderer is trying to commit their crime and the detective is trying to figure out what the barnacles is going on.

- When the murderer finds one of their victims they need to tap them on the shoulder and the victim must freeze and remain silent.

- When another player comes across a person standing silently alone they ask, 'Are you dead?' The person has to tell the truth by silently nodding or shaking their head. If they nod, the person who found them shouts, 'Murder in the Dark!'

- At this point the lights go on, the game stops and everyone returns to the room they started in.

- Next, the game moves into the courtroom, where the detective sits in a chair with the victims sat on the floor behind him and all the other players on the floor in front. If the detective (the person who picked the jack card) has been murdered then the person who picked the king card is the detective. If both those with the jack and king cards have been murdered then the person who picked the queen card is the detective.

- The detective must now try to work out who the murderer is by asking lots of questions to each person. The questions should be along the lines of, 'Where were you when "Murder in the Dark!" was called?' or, 'What have you got to say in your defence?' or, 'Who do you think the murderer is?'

- When the detective has completed their investigations they must make an informed guess as to who they think the murderer is. If asked if they are the murderer, it's vital that players answer the question truthfully.

- A winning murderer is one who avoids being identified until the bitter end.

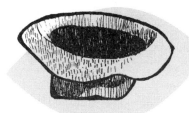

Potato Race

What's the game?

Another one that's highly amusing to watch. As the kids are blindfolded you just need to make sure they don't get too eager with their potato-foraging and smack into each other.

What do I need to play it?

A sack of potatoes and a blindfold and bucket per pair. You probably need around eight potatoes per player. If you want to prevent the kids getting mucky then I'd give the potatoes a quick scrub to get all the mud off, and dry them out first.

How many kids?

Great for smaller groups but you really need an even number. Four or six is perfect.

How do I play it?

- First of all, set up your course by scattering the potatoes in front of the competitors.
- Next, get the kids to pair up and put a blindfold on one of each of the pairs.
- On the word 'Go!' the blindfolded children must race around to grab as many potatoes as they can while their partners shout out directions. When their arms are full they race to the buckets and drop them in before carrying on again.
- Once all the potatoes are collected the pair with the most in their bucket wins.

TEN

The Organised Fun Olympics

Hosting an event devoted entirely to organised fun is the ultimate in fun-worshipping decadence. From weekends away in the country to a Christmas family holiday, with an Olympic-style event on the agenda boredom will be banished and left at home with the television.

The first time we held such an occasion was at my friend Paddy's house. As there was a gathering of twenty of us, we decided to instigate a team activity to prevent everyone straggling off into smaller, cliquey groups. We all nominated a 'sport' and ten were chosen: five to be played on the Saturday and the remaining five on the following day. From Water Torture to Competitive Yoga Posing, the weekend was one giggling array of frivolity.

We held our latest annual Olympic event while on a New Year's holiday in Crackington Haven, Cornwall. The frosty winds and sapphire sky provided the perfect backdrop to Flotsam and Jetsam Boules and Kebab Skewer Darts (see Chapter Three: Organised Fun for the Beach or Campsite for full game details).

The time of year and age and agility of your participants will determine the type of games you choose. To give you an idea, I've included a selection of games that are ideal for a weekend in the sunny outdoors. Whatever form your event takes, you should easily be able to make a selection from other chapters in this book to create an extravaganza to suit your occasion.

You can score your event by awarding gold, silver and bronze medals, or use a points-based system where extra points are awarded for special efforts, such as tugging the towel out of an opponent's hands in the Tug of Towel competition.

The Organised Fun Olympics

Recycle Bin Sculpture

What's the game?

Creative crafting from the contents of your recycling bin needn't be confined to *Blue Peter* viewers. An afternoon on a rug in the garden recreating the Angel of the North can be mightily entertaining.

What do I need to play it?

A selection of packaging and odds and sods from your recycling bin, some scissors, tape, string, drawing pins with the bendy-back bits, and some good old-fashioned glue.

How do I play it?

- Gather a good collection of recyclable bits. I'd suggest you have around four to five for each player.
- On the word 'Go!' players scrabble to collect their chosen pieces and head off to get crafting. I'd suggest putting a time limit on this event, or if you're looking for masterpieces perhaps the judging could form part of the end-of-weekend awards ceremony.
- Selection of winners is based on whatever criteria you feel are most appropriate to your group.

Competitive Yoga Posing

What's the game?

Competitive Yoga Posing will have a certain appeal to yoga enthusiasts, but it's equally entertaining to watch yoga virgins attempting to throw and hold a strong move; or indeed for the group to come up with entirely new poses of their own creation. The object of the game is to throw the most impressive but stable yoga position and challenge the other contestants to be the first to pull out. Points can be awarded for dexterity and flexibility as well as endurance, but it's easier to play 'first man down is out'. My friend Amy came up with this one for the first ever Olympic organised fun event. It was also a key feature at our most recent Olympics, with my friend Dudgey winning despite being a stonking eight months pregnant. Pretty damn impressive.

What do I need to play it?

A judge and some competitors.

'Tree'

'Half Moon'

How do I play it?

- Players form a circle and take it in turns to throw their chosen yoga move. Everyone must then copy that move. They might choose a Downward Dog, Warrior, or, if you're feeling brave, the Headstand.

- You need to make sure your moves are as challenging as possible, otherwise there will just be a lot of standing around in funny positions.

- The first person to fall out of the position is out, and it's then on to the next person, until the last person standing wins.

'Warrior'

 'Eagle'

Egg and Spoon Race

What's the game?

My sisters and I took the competitive opportunities presented at the local village fête very seriously. It was a chance for us to prove who was truly 'best' and, ever since Rachel beat the local Women's Institute in the cake-baking competition, stakes were pretty high.

I always had great hopes for our dog, Prince, winning the agility classes, and invested a lot of time in dragging him around my home-made assault course. But, as a dog with a roving eye, his preoccupation with a saucy spaniel left me red-faced at the starting line when he saw his moment to make a move. Thankfully, the day wasn't a complete write-off. Some intense practising for the Egg and Spoon Race saw me storming across the finish line as a winner.

This game does what it says on the tin: players each race to the finish line with an egg balanced on a spoon.

What do I need to play it?

An egg and spoon per player and a clear space to hold a race.

How do I play it?

- Get racers lined up at the starting line with their eggs (boiled or not, depending on how much mess you want to make) balanced on their spoons.
- On the word 'Go!' contestants race to the finish line. If their egg falls off the spoon they must go back to the starting line and begin again.
- First across is the winner.

The Organised Fun Olympics

The Blindfolded Ankle Race

What's the game?

This one's not for pregnant ladies or those with a tendency towards dizzy spells. A normal blindfolded race is made more complicated when contestants must hold their ankles as they race towards the finishing line.

What do I need to play it?

A blindfold per player, and enough room to have a race.

How do I play it?

- Get contestants blindfolded and lined up at the starting line, bent over so they're holding their ankles. Racers have the option to adopt a forward-facing or backward-facing approach.
- On the word 'Go!' contestants attempt to race towards where they think the finish line is, while maintaining a hold on their ankles. You'll need a judge to shout 'Stop!' when the first three are across the finish line and to redirect anyone who's heading for the garden pond.
- If holding your ankles is all a bit too dizzying, you can change the format to a Blindfolded Backwards Running Race.

Balloon Relay Race

What's the game?

This game is great for indoors in a big room or out in the sunny garden. Players form teams and race each other while flapping a newspaper at a balloon to make it go towards their teammate.

What do I need to play it?

A balloon and newspaper per team.

How do I play it?

- Get contestants into teams. I'd recommend no more than six people in each one. Get them to split up so half are at one end of the track and half at the other.
- The first person in each team to race holds the newspaper and balloon in front of them.
- On the word 'Go!' they flap the newspaper to create a draught that drives the balloon towards their teammates on the other side. As balloons are full of air they have a tendency to veer off course. It's harder than you might imagine it to be.
- As soon as they get their balloon to where their team member is standing at the other end of the track, the newspaper is handed over and the next person continues the race.
- The first team across the line wins.

Wheelbarrow Relay

What's the game?

Being the barrow in a wheelbarrow race is a short straw akin to being stuck at the back end of the pantomime horse. You're bound to end up with a sprained wrist or a mouthful of dirt. Quite how it's got past the health and safety police to be a regular feature at school sports days, I don't know. Needless to say, play with caution.

What do I need to play it?

Nothing but yourselves.

How do I play it?

- Mark out your racetrack. I'd suggest no more than 75 metres, otherwise you're going to break your contestants before your Olympic event is over.
- Get everyone into pairs and get them to argue and agree who's going to be the barrow.
- Once done, they all line up at the start, with the runner holding their barrow's ankles so that they're walking along on their hands.
- On the word 'Go! players race to the finishing line. First across wins.

100-Metre Roly-Poly

What's the game?

This is exactly what it sounds like. Neck-strain injuries are a potential hazard. Reduce race length to 50 metres if you're worried.

Three-Legged Race

What's the game?

There is a definite technique and an art of partnership to winning a Three-Legged Race. It's all about being able to match each other's strides and glide effortlessly to the finishing line. Make sure you partner with someone your own size if you want to have any chance of success.

The alternative, of course, is to handicap every pair by partnering them with someone of a completely different size.

What do I need to play it?

Something to tie the runners' legs together. A pair of tights is best as they have a degree of elasticity, which is useful to prevent chaffing.

How do I play it?

- Get everyone to partner up, issue each pair with a pair of tights, get them to stand side by side and strap their inside legs together.
- Mark out your designated racetrack.
- On the word 'Go!' contestants race to the finish line.

Tug of Towel

What's the game?

This is a simpler version of Tug of War, where two players compete to tug their opponent out of a circle.

What do I need to play it?

A towel – any size will do – and something to mark out your playing area.

How do I play it?

- Mark out the circle the opponents will compete in. I'd suggest ensuring it's at least three metres in diameter. If you're playing on the beach just draw one in the sand, but elsewhere you might need a piece of rope or something similar.
- The two opponents then stand in the middle and grasp the diagonally opposite corners of the towel.
- On the word 'Go!' contestants attempt to pull their opponent out of the circle to win.
- If you're using a points-based system, you might want to give extra points to contestants who manage to tug the towel out of their opponent's hands.

Longest Handstand

What's the game?

Depending on the agility of your group, you can choose to play this against a wall or not. I'd try to programme this one into the morning's itinerary. Post-lunch or post-tipple handstands could end up a bit messy.

What do I need to play it?

Strong arms, the confidence to fling yourself upside down and enough space to play in. Oh, and a stopwatch if contestants are doing their handstands separately.

How do I play it?

- This event is best played with contestants performing their manoeuvres simultaneously. If space is at a premium then I'd suggest timing each contestant to ensure a fair field of play.
- Contestants compete to see who can hold their handstand the longest, with wall or without.

Cartwheel Continuum

What's the game?

OK, I know females are likely to have an advantage with this one, but you could also say that about men and the Tug of Towel or some of the other events. This is one for flexible, free-wheeling friends. Players compete to see how many consecutive cartwheels they can achieve.

What do I need to play it?

Some safe space outdoors, i.e. not near a cliff or road, and ideally on grass.

How do I play it?

- Contestants line up at the start and on the word 'Go!' race to the finish line by seeing how many consecutive cartwheels they can do.
- Cartwheelers mustn't pause for more than three seconds in between each one; if they do, the cartwheels they have done up to that point are not counted.
- The contestant with the most cartwheels wins.

Kebab Skewer Javelin

What's the game?

Another one that won't get approved if health and safety officers are sniffing around. Needless to say, play with caution.

What do I need to play it?

Some kebab skewers. We've always found that those metal ones you get in supermarkets or camping shops work best, but if you do have the wooden sticks or posh heavy iron ones, then have a crack with them. I'm sure they all work just as well – it just means a different style of throwing.

How do I play it?

- Mark out a line in the ground.
- Contestants compete to see who can throw their kebab skewer the farthest.
- You can play it so a successful lob is only recorded if the skewer actually sticks in the ground, as this adds a certain challenge to the event.
- Farthest recorded throw wins.

Arcadia's Leap

What's the game?

We invented this at a friend's birthday on Hampstead Heath. It's great for picnics and other outdoor social occasions.

What do I need to play it?

A spacehopper is a great addition, but by no means essential.

How do I play it?

- This is a game of trust as well as jumping ability, as contestants compete to see who can jump over the most friends. Very few rules apply and any jumping style can be adopted.
- Get your first friend to lie on the ground and the contestant leaps over them.
- On each successful jump, another player lies next to their friend, making the distance to be jumped farther and farther.
- The contestant who jumps the farthest wins.
- When we played it up on the heath the birthday girl had been given a spacehopper and we used it to give us extra bounce. If you can rustle one up from somewhere, it's a definite addition to the game.

ELEVEN

Grown-Up Organised Fun for Car Journeys

The monotony of the motorway is one of life's necessary evils and, until they iron out the glitches surrounding teleporting technology, it's a fact that's unlikely to change any time soon.

With a spot of positive reframing, however, car journeys can be seen in a very different light. Instead of a grind that must be borne, they can become precious time for bonding and reconnecting. A rare opportunity for family time together. And with a bit of imagination and some good ideas up your sleeve, they can become as much fun as the holiday itself.

The games in this chapter have been designed for the older child or kidult. Needless to say, these are for the passengers. The driver's eyes and mind need to be kept strictly on the road.

Grown-Up Fun for Car Journeys

Sing-Song Ping-Pong

What's the game?

This is a well-worn game that's entertained us for many a mile. I've included it in the car section as the acoustics produced when sitting in a metal container can be pretty impressive.

This game has nothing to do with singing talents. As my friends would delight in telling you, I very rarely sing in key, but such trivial details don't hold me back from belting one out with gusto.

What do I need to play it?

Your singing voices – good or otherwise – and a pen and paper to keep scores.

How many friends?

Ideal for two to four as it gets harder with any more.

How do I play it?

- Decide who's going first, and that person sings a line from a song.
- The rest of the group must then think of another song that features any of the words that have just been sung. For example, if I was to sing, 'Golden brown, texture like **sun**,' the rest of the group would have to find another song that featured any of those words, for example, 'Don't let the **sun** go **down** on me,' then perhaps followed with the next person singing, 'Things will be great when you're **down** town, don't wait a minute more . . .'. I'm sure you get the idea.
- Players then score a point each time they correctly sing the connecting line. I'd suggest having a nominated person to keep a track of scores. It's impossible to do when you're racking your brain for song lines.

Sing Your Way through the Alphabet

What's the game?

This one's an adaptation of the game above, but instead of matching a word you have to sing songs whose titles work through the alphabet. You might start with 'Away in a Manger', the classic Christmas carol, before moving on to 'Blowin' in the Wind' by Bob Dylan. Points awarded as before, each time the player comes up with the next sequential song.

Spoof

What's the game?

This is a simple guessing game in which players guess the total number of coins everyone holds in their hands.

What do I need to play it?

Three coins per player.

How many friends?

Ideal for between two and five.

How do I play it?

- Players are each given three coins and on the count of three hold one, two or all of them in an outstretched fist, all pointing towards each other.
- Players then take it in turns to guess the total number of coins that are held in all fists. Two players can't make the same bid. The player with the closest number is saved and the remaining players play another round, while the person with the guess that is farthest away loses a life or is out.

Pub Cricket

What's the game?

This game is ideal if you're driving around country roads in Britain, as it requires you to spot that very British thing: a country pub.

What do I need to play it?

A car journey on some country roads.

How many friends?

A car full. You're mildly disadvantaged if you're sat in the middle.

How do I play it?

- Players take it in turns to go in to bat.
- If they pass a pub when they're in play, they get a point for every leg on the pub sign. The Black Dog, for example, would get four points, whereas The Eagle would only score two. The highest score I know of was when Barney's cousin Tom spotted a pub called The Grand Old Duke of York. The duke and his ten thousand men scored him 22,002 points in one hit.
- The end of your innings is when you pass a pub that doesn't feature any legs, for example The Star and Garter.
- The game stops at the end of the journey and the person with the highest score wins.

Mousehole

What's the game?

For those familiar with the Radio 4 show *I'm Sorry I Haven't a Clue*, the game Mornington Crescent requires little introduction. Mornington Crescent is a feature of the show that's famous for its incredibly complicated rules. It's believed to have been invented by the panel as a way to fox an unpopular producer, as the rules are never fully explained and leave outsiders befuddled and bemused.

I recently came across an old book on parlour games and found Mornington Crescent listed as the following game, with Mousehole as an alternative title. Whether these are its true origins I'm not entirely sure, but there are indeed some minor similarities. Either way, this game lacks the complexities of the Radio 4 version and should provide some entertainment for a good hour.

Mousehole is a Victorian parlour game where players take it in turns to pick a place name, and the next player must respond by nominating another one that starts with the letter the previous one ended with.

What do I need to play it?

Just yourselves and a pad and pen to keep score.

How many friends?

A car full.

How do I play it?

- The aim of the game is to respond to a player calling out a British town by matching it with another one starting with the letter the previous ended in, for example, Derby, York, Kettering . . .

- Players must avoid choosing a place which ends in M, such as Cobham, as this would allow the next player to say 'Mousehole!' and therefore win.

- It's good to choose town names where the spelling is slightly questionable as this will hoodwink fellow players into getting it wrong.

- If a player does get it wrong, they are out. The winner is either the last one left, or the first to be able to say 'Mousehole!'

Grown-Up Fun for Car Journeys

- You can change the category used for the game. For example, it might be stations on the underground or capital cities around the world, or something that's relevant to you.

Dirty Doubles

What's the game?

My friends Beth and John came up with this game on one particularly long and arduous journey. We were heading down to a festival on a Friday afternoon and were stuck in traffic as the sun beat down. The radio didn't work and the music selection was particularly dire, but we were blessed with a wide variety of audio books to entertain the children travelling with us. While the kids giggled their way through stories of wizards and wands, unbeknownst to them we developed our own game that entertained us at a rather more base level.

What do I need to play it?

An audio book. Harry Potter's wand-laden tales are perfect.

How many friends?

As many as are in the car.

How do I play it?

- Get your audio book on and playing nice and loud for everyone to hear.
- The objective of the game is to spot the dirty double entendres that are unconsciously woven into the tale.
- Each successful spot scores a point.

Get Lost

What's the game?

This is one to play when you've got some time on your hands, and definitely not when you're setting off with a clear destination in mind. It quite simply involves writing out some farcical directions and following them to see where they take you. The best destination wins. Oh, and you need to be somewhere none of you know your way around for it to work properly.

A friend and I came up with the game when we were travelling in India, and it was undoubtedly the making of the trip. We'd hired one of those old Enfields and decided to head off the well-worn traveller track to escape the harassing hawkers and braying gap-year students. For a whole week, we took it in turns to write out the directions for the day and set off through rice fields, past spice farms and into rural villages, where our arrival was met with a mixture of trepidation and delight. Each afternoon we'd stop the game in the first village we came to and pay a few rupees to use a family's floor for the night. My friend won the game when he managed to guide us down a rutted track and into the yard of a rural family home. The hospitality we received that day is something I'll always remember. They slaughtered one of their goats and prepared a feast that went on well into the night, with the gathered goat herders teaching us to dance their local dance.

What do I need to play it?

Some pen, paper, a car and some time on your hands.

How many friends?

Works brilliantly with two of you, or however many of you are in the car.

How do I play it?

- Each write out a set of made-up directions that involve, for example: 'Second left, first right . . .' and so on. Leave out things like roundabouts or 'left at the church', as you'd be overly lucky if they were to appear.
- Follow the directions, and the one who set out the route to the best destination wins.

Thumb Wars

What's the game?

Popular in school playgrounds across Britain, this one retains its fun value for adults. Cars are a good place to play it as the confined space will stop the game getting too out of hand. It's often used to decide who's going to do something, such as who is going to be 'it'. Can also be used to identify who's buying coffees at the next pit stop.

What do I need to play it?

Strong thumbs.

How many friends?

Two play at a time, but run it as a tournament if there are more of you in the car. Driver is most definitely excluded from this one.

How do I play it?

- Face your opponent and hook all fingers of one hand with your opponent, leaving the thumb pointing upwards as if you're doing a thumbs up.

- Next, move your thumbs over and under each other's while still remaining linked in by your fingers, and repeat the following rhyme:

    One, two, three, four,
    I declare a thumb war.

- After the word 'war', players must battle to be the one to squash their opponent's thumb by pushing and holding it down with theirs for three seconds.

- The thumb-squashing player is the winner.

Double Back

What's the game?

Another one to convert motorway mundanity into a playground of verbal fun. A working knowledge of *Hello!* magazine or similar titles will give you a definite advantage.

What do I need to play it?

A sound knowledge of famous or infamous people or characters.

How many friends?

Works really well with between two and eight people.

How do I play it?

- The objective of the game is to come up with characters' or actors' names that use the first letter of the surname of the one the previous person has stated, and if possible come up with a character who has the same letters beginning their first and surnames.

- You can vary the rules to state that players must only choose living actors, or you might choose to have anarchy and allow any individual to be named, famous or non-famous, fictional or real. I'd recommend you have a time limit on each person's go. We normally allow ten seconds.

- The first person says an actor's or character's name.

- The next person to go must find a name that starts with the same letter as the surname of the previously mentioned character. For example, if I was to mention Simon Cowell, the next player must choose a name that begins with C such as Carol Vorderman.

- Or, you can try to come up with a character whose first name and surname start with the same letter, for example, if the previous character's surname ended in an M, you could choose Marilyn Monroe. When you do, this sends the game back in the other direction.

- A character can only be mentioned once.

- If you can't go within the agreed timeframe, you're out.

- Last player in wins.

Scissor Paper Stone

What's the game?

Everyone knows this one and I'm sure there are a million and one variations. It should entertain you all in the back of the car for at least ten minutes and is another fine way to decide who's paying for petrol or buying treats at the next pit stop.

What do I need to play it?

Just your hands.

How many friends?

A car full.

How do I play it?

- Form a fist with your hand, and on the count of three form the shape of either a pair of scissors, a piece of paper or a stone, and hold your hand shape out in front of you.

- The rules of the game are that the shape you form will either defeat or be defeated by the other players. Scissors cut paper but are blunted by stone, and paper wraps stone.

- Other variations include earth, fire and water, or any others you might want to come up with.

Hestia

What's the game?

This is the sort of game that your English teacher might have got you to play on the last day of term. Mildly challenging and great to prevent the deterioration of your brain into worthless holiday mush.

What do I need to play it?

A good grasp of the English language.

How many friends?

A car load of them is spot on.

How do I play it?

- The first player to go chooses a homophone (a word that has different spellings and meanings which all sound the same). A few examples are air or heir, lie or lye, farther or father, made or maid, son or sun, for, fore or four, stair or stare, storey or story, one or won, bridal or bridle – hopefully you get the idea.
- Next, they start to tell a story that features this word in its different forms without actually mentioning it.
- If, for example, a player's chosen word was 'bank', they then might tell a story about the sides of a river and the place that looks after your money. For example: 'One day, Jeremy the bear left his house, walked along one side of the river and into town, hoping to take some money out . . .'. The objective of the game is that you must do this without actually mentioning the word 'bank', leaving this for fellow players to guess. I'd weave a complicated tale in there to prevent it from being too obvious.
- As soon as a fellow player has guessed what the word is, they join in to converse on the subject. The last one to join in loses.

Just a Minute

What's the game?

Just like its famous Radio 4 namesake, this game requires players to keep talking on a subject for sixty seconds. The game is believed to have been invented by Ian Messiter when riding on the top deck of the number 13 bus. He remembered being petrified at being asked by one of his schoolmasters to talk non-stop for one minute and immediately recognised its entertainment potential if played with erudite and articulate friends.

What do I need to play it?

Some sharp-talking wits about you and pen and paper.

How many friends?

Two to six is best.

How do I play it?

- All players write down five topics of conversation, which are then folded up and put in someone's hat or a similar vessel.
- Players take it in turns to pull a topic from the hat, and then speak on the subject for a minute without hesitation, deviation or repeating a word, with the exception of mentioning the given subject.
- Points are awarded when other players make a correct challenge for perceived hesitations, deviation or repetition. I'd suggest nominating a non-playing umpire to prevent arguments occurring.

Window Messages

What's the game?

I can already hear the rumblings of complaints that will roll in from various quarters on this one. If you take it with a big fat pinch of salt you'll see the amusement factor. This is for passengers only. Driver, keep your eyes on the road.

What do I need to play it?

Plain paper and thick marker pens.

How many friends?

Everyone in the car excluding the driver.

How do I play it?

- Everyone in the car decides on an appropriate and definitely not rude phrase that should be communicated to passengers in other vehicles.
- It might be, 'Can I come in your car instead?' or, ' Our car's better than yours.'
- Decide on a victim in another car who is not the driver, and everyone then has to guess what their response to the note is going to be.
- When you're ready, hold the note up to be seen by the non-driver in the other car.
- Whoever guesses the right response scores a point.

Grown-Up Fun for Car Journeys

Just Say No

What's the game?

This game is about interrogation. I've always found car journeys to be a brilliant way to catch up or properly quiz a friend, particularly on a subject they're uncomfortable talking about. It must be something to do with how easily eye contact is avoided as you stare out to the road, and there are always a wealth of opportunities such as, 'Ooh, shall we try the B1393 instead?' to tactically change the subject.

What do I need to play it?

An inquisitive mind and some topics to cover.

How many friends?

Everyone in the car.

How do I play it?

- The rules are that players mustn't say 'Yes' or 'No' when under one minute's intense interrogation. The only other rule is that they must always tell the truth.

- Players take it in turns to be victim while everyone else around bombards them with questions to try to force them to say 'Yes' or 'No'.

- If they make it to the end without messing up, they get a point. All questions must be answered, and there's a ten-second penalty for a hesitation.

TWELVE

Kids' Organised Fun for Car Journeys

We've all been there. Stuck in a car with a fidgeting, scrapping, crying pack of kids. Games, as any well-travelled parent will know, are the most valued tools available. It's a dead cert that during any journey of over one hour interludes of pure hell will be endured. As children can be known to demonstrate Lucifer-like traits under these circumstances, it is recommended that you come armed with a wide variety and a few winners up your sleeve.

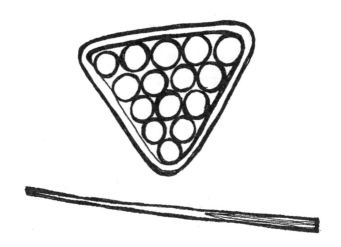

Wotsit Sculptures

What's the game?

My packed lunches were wholewheat drudgery when I was a child. I think my mum must have been going through a 'yoghurt knitting' hippy stage at the time, as the only brand that ever appeared in my lunch box was a mini packet of raisins as a treat.

On Sundays after church, I got my 25p pocket money, which was spent in pursuit of a sugar rush served up at the local corner shop. As I also wanted to get a copy of *The Beano*, it often meant a tough decision between entertainment or treacly delights. By chance, I discovered that Wotsits provided both for the price of one. These cheesy snacks soon became my nibble of choice when I realised the fun that could be had from creating Day-Glo orange sculptures.

Now I'm attempting to board the healthy eating bandwagon, and as such recommend substituting Wotsits for those vegetable puff crisps. All the fun without the calories (and whatever it takes to create that Day-Glo orange colour).

What do I need to play it?

A packet of healthy vegetable puff crisps per child. It only works with puffed-style crisps.

How many young friends?

As many as want to play.

How do I play it?

- The object of the game is to craft the most creative and impressive sculpture out of Wotsits.
- To sculpt using Wotsits, simply bite the top off one of them, lick it and stick another one on top. A bit of pressure will ensure a durable piece of craftsmanship.
- Best one wins.

A to Z

What's the game?

This is another one to roll out on a long and tedious journey. You'll at first be delighted by its ability to engage kids for hours and be played again and again, before it drives you slowly around the bend. It involves listing the A to Z of items in a specific category, whether it's types of chairs or breeds of dog . . . oh, the list is truly endless.

What do I need to play it?

A fast-thinking brain, that ideally holds a full working knowledge of the *Encyclopaedia Britannica*.

How many young friends?

As many as are in the car.

How do I play it?

- Split into two teams and take it in turns to nominate a category for the opposing team, who then have to list items in that category from A to Z. If the chosen category was cars, you might start with Aston Martin, followed by BMW, and so on.
- Each go runs until the team can't think of an item that corresponds to the next letter. Points are awarded for the number of items they correctly come up with.
- This one's great for older kids, but just make sure your team split partners any youngsters with an adult.

Farm Wars

What's the game?

This one's meant for young kids. Points are awarded for animals that are spotted along the way. It's best played on country roads as the speed of a motorway makes it tricky to identify what's in each field.

What do I need to play it?

A car travelling on a relatively slow road.

How many young friends?

As many kids as you have in your car.

How do I play it?

- Half the car is on cows and the other half is on sheep. You score one point for each field of cows or sheep that you pass. If you pass a cemetery, you lose all your points.

- You can then make up additional points based on the journey that you're making. If you're travelling through an urban area, you might award a point if you spot someone walking a dog, and if you can get that person to wave to you, you score five points.

Animal, Mineral, Vegetable

What's the game?

I've got a misty memory of playing this as a child, though we sometimes called it Twenty Questions, from what I can remember. This Victorian parlour game involves trying to guess what the other person is thinking of with only twenty 'yes or no' questions. Its adult entertainment value is fairly limited, but it's great for engaging kids.

What do I need to play it?

Nothing.

How many young friends?

Works best in smaller groups of kids, aged five and upwards.

How do I play it?

- Take it in turns to play. The first person thinks of something and the rest of the players try to guess what it is by asking twenty questions that only get 'yes' or 'no' answers. The first question is 'Is it an animal?' Then if it's a 'no' the next person asks 'Is it a mineral?' Finally, if still a 'no', 'Is it a vegetable?' Subsequent questions might be 'Does it have wings?' or 'Is it edible?'
- As soon as the answer is guessed, it moves on to be the next person's turn.

Better Letter

What's the game?

This is another winner for confined spaces and has the added advantage of working for adults as well as kids. Children need to be old enough to have a strong vocabulary and a good grasp of spelling. The game involves slowly building a word letter by letter, with players trying not to be the person who adds the last letter.

What do I need to play it?

Nothing.

How many young friends?

A car full.

How do I play it?

- The aim of the game is to create a word by taking it in turns to add the next letter. Whoever is obliged to add the final letter loses the game.
- So, for example, say the first few letters that were in turn selected were C, R, E, A, T, and so on, for the beginnings of a word that builds on 'creat'. Players can then choose to direct it to become 'creative', or 'creation', or even 'creature', depending on which word ensures they're not left with the last letter when it comes back around to them.

Silly Sentences

What's the game?

This game is basically Consequences Lite; great for kids of all ages who've learnt how to talk. The younger the child, the more entertaining it should end up being, and again it's another one that also works for adults.

What do I need to play it?

Nothing.

How many friends?

At least two of you.

How do I play it?

- In this game, players make up coherent sentences by taking it in turns to contribute a word, for example, 'Sarah,' 'Hated,' 'Salami,' and so on. . .
- Kids love to drag this one out to create stupidly daft and long sentences.
- Ideally you want the game to play with a bit of pace, and once they start getting good, get them to move on to a mini-story.

Car Snooker

What's the game?

This game will keep your kids occupied and staring out of the window for hours. It's the same points system as for snooker, but instead of potting the balls they're spotting the cars.

What do I need to play it?

You need to be travelling on a road with a fair amount of traffic. Doesn't work as well in quiet country lanes. It's also a good idea to have a pad and pen to keep track of scores, and a stopwatch of some sort to time each round.

How many young friends?

A car full.

How do I play it?

- Each player has two minutes, which is timed by the parent up front.
- If they spot a red car when it's their go they score one point, and a black scores seven. For those not familiar with the game of snooker, the points are detailed below:

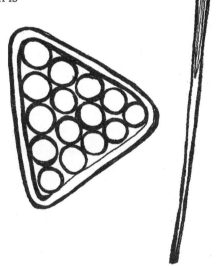

  - A red car = one point.
  - A yellow car = two points.
  - A green car = three points.
  - A brown car or any lorry = four points.
  - A blue car = five points.
  - A pink car = six points.
  - A black car = seven points.
- The player with the highest score at the end of the journey wins.

Alphabet Signs

What's the game?

This is great for young kids who are learning to read and write.

What do I need to play it?

A road with lots of easily readable signs. Motorways and well-signposted cities are perfect. You might struggle to play it with any effect on country lanes.

How many young friends?

All those in the car.

How do I play it?

- The objective is to spot a road sign beginning with the next sequential letter in the alphabet.
- So, for example, someone might spot a sign to Andover followed by another spot of a sign beginning with B such as Brick Lane. Clearly, this is hypothetical.

Alphabet Car Plates

What's the game?

As above, but this time players spot car number plates beginning with sequential alphabet letters. Another fun use of car plates is to take the final three letters of a plate and try to come up with the funniest phrase or name, for example, CBH could be Charles Boothby-Helicopter, or Cows Breathe Heavily . . .

The Animal Impression Game

What's the game?

Now for some reason I was rather fond of this game at university. It probably paints me as a rather odd young lady, but I was particularly proud of the farmyard impersonations I'd developed and perfected after spending much of my childhood helping out on a Devonshire farm.

Kids love this game as it allows them to be as noisy and giggly as they like.

How many young friends?

As many as are in the car.

What do I need to play it?

Children with a good knowledge of animals and the noises they make.

How do I play it?

- Each child takes it in turns to do an impression of an animal of their choice, and the other children have to guess what it is. If they guess correctly, it's then their turn. As you might imagine, it's fun to attempt difficult animals such as iguanas and giraffes . . .
- If they don't manage to come up with one then they're out.
- Last child in is the winner.

THIRTEEN

Poolside Organised Fun

Swimming pools offer a plethora of fun-making opportunities. There's only so much swimming up and down that can be done before boredom or even fatigue sets in, and you need a reason to stay in the pool so you're out of the sun.

A whole chapter has thus been devoted to pool-based entertainment. Many of the games require you to take over the whole pool, so if you're playing in a shared holiday swimming pool, I'd suggest taking a leaf out of Peter Cooke's book (see page 278) and encouraging and cajoling other hotel guests to join in.

Marco Polo

What's the game?

Marco Polo is a game of poolside 'It' that's become popular around the world. The rules vary depending on the size of your pool and where it's being played, but generally it involves someone scrabbling around with their eyes closed trying to catch their fellow players.

The origins of the name have nothing to do with a popular clothing brand, but instead refer to an intrepid medieval Italian explorer of the mysteries of the East.

What do I need to play it?

A swimming pool and some energetic friends.

How many friends?

A minimum of three, or as many of you as can fit in the swimming pool.

How do I play it?

- Decide who's going to be 'it'. They close their eyes and count to ten while the rest of the players scatter around the pool.

- The person who's 'it' then proceeds to swim around the pool with their eyes closed to try to catch their friends, who are also moving about.

- To give a clue as to their whereabouts, the person who's 'it' can shout out 'Marco!' and the rest of the players must respond with 'Polo!'

- As soon as another player is caught, it's their turn to be 'it'.

- Another variation allows players to climb out of the water when they're not it to prevent them being caught. If the person who's 'it' shouts out 'Fish out of water!' while someone's out of the pool, this means they become 'it'. If there are lots of people out of the water, the person who's 'it' can choose who becomes 'it' next. If there's no one out of the water when they shout, the person who's 'it' has to do the counting part all over again.

- Another additional rule is that if the person who's 'it' shouts out 'Alligator eyes!' they're allowed to swim under the water with their eyes open to have a good look at where everyone is.

Peter Cooke's Egyptian pool game

What's the game?

I came across this game in a book about the legendary Peter Cooke featuring a collection of stories from some of his friends and colleagues. Stephen Fry, my one and only celebrity idol, had written about a game Peter Cooke had invented while on a Nile cruise organised by the very generous John Cleese.

One searingly hot afternoon while on a hotel stop-off on the way to the Egyptian monument of Abu Simbel, guests were resting in the shade out of the way of the blistering heat. Meanwhile Peter Cooke was striding up and down eyeing up the pool set-up with a beach ball tucked under each arm. After some time he stood at one end of the pool and rolled one of his balls along the edge towards the hooped handle of the pool steps and as the ball rolled through the hoop, glancing off the left-hand upright he shouted, 'Aaah a Rufford – two points.' The rest of the guests, tiring of their books began to look on bemused. He rolled again and this time the ball got stuck in between the posts, 'Strottled, damn it, one point.' With their interest now roused, one of the guests asked, 'What happens if it rolls straight through?' his quick reply, 'A clean Abu Simbel of course – five points. And a Trote, when the ball clears but lands in the water is minus two, with retrieval duty.'

Before long, books were downed and guests had joined Peter to play in what turned into a highly competitive and tense afternoon of Abu Simbel. Soon the gathering had caught the attention of the other hotel guests and staff and before long an international tournament was organised culminating in the winning team being awarded a vase pilfered by Peter Cooke from his hotel room.

What do I need to play it?

A beach ball and a swimming pool with either pool steps that feature a hooped handle or a chair that can be positioned by the pool to create the same effect.

278

How many friends?

As many as are around to play.

How do I play it?

- Divide yourselves into teams of around five on each side and identify your goal posts or position a chair by the side of the pool to create the same effect.
- The aim of the game is to be the first team to reach twenty points. Each player has two bowls or 'Strives' as Peter named them.
- A reminder of scoring as follows:
  - A Rufford: when the beach ball clears through the hoop, glances off to one side but doesn't actually go in the water – two points.
  - Strottled: when the ball gets stuck in between the posts – one point.
  - A Trote: when the ball clears but lands in the water resulting in retrieval duty by the offending player – minus two.
  - Abu Simbel: when the ball clears the hoop and passes on through – five points.

You can of course devise a scoring and naming system to suit your pool environment and as long as the game is played in honour of the legend himself, I'm sure he would approve.

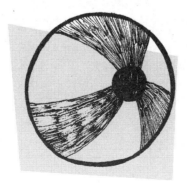

Water Cricket

What's the game?

This game is a cross between Baseball and Cricket, played in a swimming pool.

What do I need to play it?

A swimming pool, a tennis ball and a bat of some sort.

How many friends?

A minimum of three, though the more the better.

How do I play it?

- Decide who's going to go in to bat first, and who will be bowler.
- The batter stands at the edge of the pool while the bowler and fielders position themselves in the water.
- The bowler bowls the ball to the batter from a distance of about one to two metres. If the batter misses the ball three times then they're out.
- To score two points, the batter has to dive into the water after hitting the ball, swim to where the bowler stands, swim back again and then climb out. To score one point, they must just jump in the water and climb back out again.
- Meanwhile, the fielders have to get the ball back to the bowler before the batter completes this movement.
- If the ball is back to the bowler before the batter is back at their base, then the batter is out and it's another player's turn to bat.
- This game continues until everybody has had a chance to bat, and scores are counted up to see who's declared the winner.

Andy's Feet First Race

What's the game?

This game was invented one summer at my friend Nick's house in France. It was another searingly hot day and Andy came up with a series of games to keep us entertained in the water. It's a novel way to race across the pool and does wonders for your stomach muscles.

What do I need to play it?

Your good swimming self and a pool to play in.

How many friends?

As many as you can fit in a race across the pool.

How do I play it?

- Racers line up, holding the side of the pool, with their feet pushed out in front of them.
- On the word 'Go!' players must swim to the other end with their feet first and their toes poking out of the water.
- Any deviation from this position is considered a foul and players must pause for three seconds before starting to swim again.

Pool Pogo

What's the game?

Another one that came from that lazy French holiday. This time, players race across the pool bouncing up and down.

What do I need to play it?

A swimming pool and some energetic friends.

How many friends?

As before. As many as you can fit in a race across the pool.

How do I play it?

- Get yourselves lined up at the side of the pool.
- On the word 'Go!' you race to the other side of the pool with your hands held behind your back, bouncing up and down.
- Racers need to ensure they touch the bottom of the pool on every bounce. This is vital to propel yourself across.

Tugadug

What's the game?

Two players in the pool try to score a penalty within a designated goal area using their hands.

What do I need to play it?

A floating ball and a swimming pool.

How many friends?

Works best with two players.

How do I play it?

- First of all, mark out your goal area by positioning bags or chairs at the edge of the pool. I'd suggest ensuring it is no more than three metres wide.
- One player goes in goal, while the other attempts to hit the side of the pool within the designated goal area by chucking the ball. A goal only counts when it's within the designated goal area and it hits the edge of the pool (not going farther behind, out of the pool).
- Each player has a set amount of shooting time and the highest scorer wins.

Dugdale's Lilo Surfing

What's the game?

I've tried this and found it impossible to achieve. As with surfing, you need to invest time and effort to crack it. If you're lucky enough to have a whole summer and regular access to a swimming pool then I reckon you might nail it.

What do I need to play it?

A swimming pool and two lilos.

How many friends?

You can play on your own, or hold a competition when you get good.

How do I play it?

- The basic idea is to surf across the pool balanced on two lilos. The person who gets the farthest wins.
- To get started, carefully balance two lilos on top of each other and position them at the side of the pool.
- Next, get out of the pool, stand about three metres back and take a running jump so that your feet land in the middle of the lilos. Your velocity then propels the lilos out into the pool. Meanwhile, you need to balance on top to get as far as you can without falling in.
- Once you've mastered the technique you can then take it to competition level to see who can get the farthest while remaining balanced on the lilos.

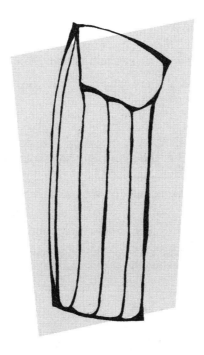

Poolside Fun

Shark

What's the game?

Piggy in the Middle rules, played in water.

What do I need to play it?

A ball and a swimming pool to play in.

How many friends?

Three of you to play, but if there are a few more you can swap over as you go.

How do I play it?

- All three of you stand in the swimming pool, with one in the middle and the other two either side.
- The two players throw the ball to each other over the head of the person in the middle.
- Meanwhile, the 'shark' in the middle has to intercept the ball as it travels across.
- If they catch it, the person who threw it is then the shark.

Whirlpool

What's the game?

You need a small pool to make this one work.

What do I need to play it?

A small swimming pool. A deep jacuzzi is perfect.

How many friends?

Four is ideal.

How do I play it?

- Players all stand at the side of the pool and start running on the spot at the same speed.
- As you get faster and faster, a whirlpool suction is created. Once a whirlpool starts to form, one player jumps in and rides down it.
- Will amuse you for a good five minutes.

FOURTEEN

Christmas-Themed Organised Fun

Every year from September onwards, the magic of Christmas is shoved down our throats, making it pretty hard to ignore. The expectation of these clove-scented scenes is often far from reality. It's more commonly a time for gritted-teeth smiles and mulled-wine strops, as surly sisters scrap over who's doing all the sprout chopping and why it's always left to you to stuff the turkey.

After Christmas feasting is done, and the sloe gin and champagne quaffing have nullified tensions and lulled everyone into an inebriated state of happiness, a game is a guaranteed reminder of kinship bonds, as you giggle behind your paper hat at your grandmother's impression of Monty Python.

According to Desmond Morris, the Tudors were responsible for carving out the tradition of games at Christmas. True to dictatorial form, the aristocracy gallantly permitted the labouring classes to join them for a yuletide games knees-up – a pastime that the ruling classes enjoyed all year round (10).

This whole book is packed full of games that are great to play at Christmas, but the following chapter features those which are Christmas themed. They've been listed in chronological order to help provide entertainment that will last you throughout the day.

Christmas Carol Relay

What's the game?

This is a seasonal adaptation of an earlier game. It's a regular accompaniment to Christmas Day preparations as we wrap our presents or stuff the turkey.

What do I need to play it?

Your best carol-singing voices and a pen and paper to keep scores.

How many friends?

Ideal for two to four people going about their Christmas chores.

How do I play it?

- Decide who's going first and get that person to sing a line from a popular Christmas carol.
- The rest of the group must then think of another song that features any of the words that have just been sung. For example, if I was to sing, 'Silent night, holy **night**, all is calm, all is bright, round yon virgin mother and child . . .', then the next player might sing, 'While shepherds watched their flocks by **night**, all seated on the ground, the **angel** of the Lord came down . . .', perhaps followed by, 'The **angel** Gabriel from heaven came . . .', and so on.

  - Players then score a point each time they correctly sing the connecting line. I'd suggest having a nominated person to keep a track of scores as it's impossible to do this when you're fishing Christmas carol lines from the back of your head.

The Huggins' Present Pie

What's the game?

This is a really fun way to distribute presents to kids. My friends Nick and John used to do this with their kids every Christmas. They got fed up with little hands poking and prodding and ruining the surprise for Christmas Day. You need to make sure your presents are small enough to fit in your box and light enough to be pulled out on a piece of string.

What do I need to play it?

A big box, lots and lots of wrapping or brown paper, string, labels, and presents for all the kids, which are small enough to fit in the box and light enough to be pulled out.

How many friends?

As many children as there are presents.

How do I play it?

- Wrap your presents up as normal, securely tie a long piece of string (about three metres) onto each of the gifts, and tie a label to the end with the person's name on it.

- Place all the presents in a big cardboard box with the lid off. Then wrap this large box so that it's entirely covered with paper, with holes at the four corners, and with one or two of the strings coming out of each hole with the labels attached to the end.

- Place this large box under the tree.

- At the appointed present-opening time, get the kids to each take hold of the piece of string with their name on it and all pull simultaneously to release the presents from the box, so that they burst through the wrapping paper and into their laps.

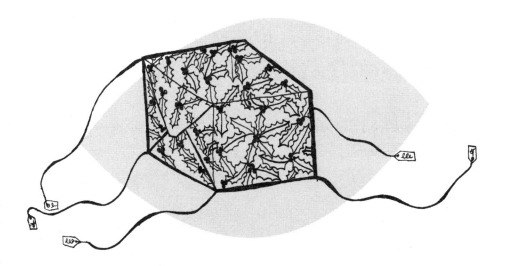

Father Christmas's Beard

What's the game?

A team race to see who can create the best Father Christmas within a set period of time.

What do I need to play it?

Lots of cotton wool balls and a pot of Vaseline per team. Chairs and a stopwatch.

How many friends?

At least four of you, and as many others as want to play.

How do I play it?

- Get everyone into teams and get the players to nominate who will be their Father Christmas.
- Father Christmas sits in the chair, with the other players surrounding him. Each team has an equal share of cotton wool balls and a pot of Vaseline each.
- On the word 'Go!' teams race to create the most recognisable Father Christmas by sticking cotton wool balls onto their nominated player's face using the Vaseline.
- Best Father Christmas after sixty seconds wins.

Human Christmas Tree

What's the game?

For when you have piles of ribbon, wrapping paper and other present packaging left at the end of Christmas – this game will put these to good use and add an element of fun to clearing it all away.

What do I need to play it?

A big, messy pile of post-present-opening debris.

How many friends?

As many or as few are sat around your tree.

How do I play it?

- Split into two teams, or three if there are a few of you. The ideal number to have in each team is three to four.

- Equally divide up all the leftover wrapping paper, ribbons and packaging so that there's a healthy pile for each team. You might want to top these up with extra Christmas decorations that you have lying around.

- Decide who's going to be the Christmas tree in each team. Teams then have five minutes to turn their elected player into the best Christmas tree, using the leftover debris.

- Prizes awarded for creative use of materials as well as closeness to the real Christmas tree form.

Character Christmas Dinner

What's the game?

Make Christmas dinner even more entertaining by inviting guests to attend in full fancy-dress regalia. Outfits can be Christmas themed or created from whatever favourite pieces people have at home.

Name That Carol

What's the game?

This is a great one to play as you while away Christmas afternoon listening to carols on the radio.

What do I need to play it?

Some Christmas carol music.

How many friends?

As many as are there.

How do I play it?

Players race to be the first to guess which Christmas carol is being played. Points are scored each time one is correctly identified.

Snow Fun

What's the game?

Have you ever been paintballing? This has the same 'capture the flag' type of principle, but played in the snow. I've featured it in the Christmas section as snow does always feel Christmassy. The likelihood of snow on Christmas Day in most parts of Britain is, of course, rather slim.

What do I need to play it?

Something to make two flags out of – two sticks and two tea towels are perfect.

How many friends?

This works best in larger groups. You really need enough for two teams, so a minimum of six players.

How do I play it?

- Get into two teams, each nominate your base and then position your flag there.
- The objective of the game is to retrieve your opponents' flag from their base without getting hit by a snowball. I'd suggest agreeing a strategy within your team to define who will be on defence and who on attack.
- Each team needs to start off at their respective base and charge across to retrieve their opponents' flag.

FIFTEEN

Organised Fun at Work

Everyone knows that work can at times be indescribably dull. Naturally it depends on what you do, but there's generally a time in everyone's week when you've done enough or you've given up for the day. You could of course be diligent and catch up on all the boring bits that swim at the bottom of your list. Failing that, you could use the time to catch up with colleagues and engage in a bit of light entertainment. A perfect time, in fact, to organise some fun.

Pad Ping-Pong

What's the game?

Quite simply, Ping-Pong using your notepads and a ball of screwed-up paper.

What do I need to play it?

Your notepads and a couple of torn sheets screwed up, or even taped into a tight ball, and a barrier to play over.

How many friends?

Works best with two of you, with someone else acting as umpire. If there are more of you that want to play then you can of course run it as a tournament-style event.

How do I play it?

- Get set up so that you're each holding a pad and have your firmly screwed-up and taped ball of paper to hand, and position yourself either side of a desk with enough room to move around.

- The rules are exactly the same as a normal game of Ping-Pong except that you lose the bounce.

- A point is awarded for each rally, and either opponent can score a point regardless of who served.

- The winner is the first to either fifteen or twenty-one points, depending on the length of game you want to play.

Work Dares

What's the game?

For those looking for a considerable distraction, Work Dares can happily consume an entire week's worth of working hours. The aim of the game is to challenge your colleagues to a series of points-based dares to determine who's the bravest of you all. You'll need a degree of confidence in your job security as, if taken too far, this one has the potential to turn sour. A gentle warning.

What do I need to play it?

An agreed set of dares, with a scoresheet to monitor progress.

How many friends?

A smaller group of two to four works best. You'll more than likely attract adverse attention along with your P45 if you play on your own.

How do I play it?

- First of all, you need to agree a set of dares and agree the points that each one carries. For example, cartwheeling through your office shouting, 'I'm so happy I just can't stop myself!' might attract two points, whereas breaking into a Thriller routine in the middle of an important meeting, I feel, should qualify for at least five.
- I've featured a number of examples under the different points segments, but I'd suggest creating some bespoke ones for your working environment.
- One-point dares:
  - Reverse your chair around your desk or, indeed, the office, as if you were reversing around the corner in your car. If anyone asks, just tell them you're practising for your advanced driving test.
  - Hop everywhere for two hours, and if anyone asks what you're doing, say it's a yoga practice technique to strengthen muscles and improve balance.

- Two-point dares:
  - Roly-poly your way to the toilet or water cooler.
  - Stand to attention, look straight ahead and bark 'Yes, Sir!' every time someone asks you something. Do this for the first ten people who speak to you.
- Three-point dares:
  - Every time someone speaks to you, at the end of the conversation look them in their eyes and say, 'I do know, but don't worry, I'm not going to mention it to a soul.' Do this to the first ten people you meet.
  - Belch loudly every time anyone speaks to you, no matter who it is, and follow it with profuse apologies that your gout is playing up.

Stationery Warfare

What's the game?

For most of us, work can lead to boredom and irritation. We all have a couple of colleagues who manage to wind us up through their ability to locate that little frustrating niggle. It's an inevitability of spending a vast percentage of our waking hours closeted in a small space with people we might otherwise not bother to say hello to. Stationery warfare is a great way to work through some of that frustration.

What do I need to play it?

Ammunition and a firing device, namely balls of screwed-up paper and a ruler each. Use paper from your recycling bin rather than wasting new sheets. It's also good to have something to act as your trench or barrier to duck behind when in the throes of war.

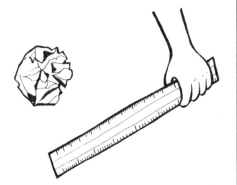

How many friends?

Between two and six people works best. It's good to have an impartial umpire who can keep scores.

How do I play it?

- Get into your teams and arm yourselves with a ruler each and a good amount of screwed-up paper ammunition, and position yourselves behind your respective team barricades.

- The aim of the game is to make as many direct hits on the opposing team as possible within a set time period. A direct hit is made by catapulting a screwed-up ball of paper at one of your opponents using your ruler.

- The team that makes the highest number of hits wins.

Pick Up Pencils

What's the game?

This is an improvisation of the popular children's game of Pick Up Sticks that can easily be played wherever you have access to the stationery cupboard.

What do I need to play it?

A packet of colouring pencils or different coloured biros.

How many friends?

Works best with two to four.

How do I play it?

- First of all, agree the points assigned to the different colours, for example, all tones of red (including pinks) are five points, tones of green are four, and so on.

- Clear a space to play in and empty your packet of colouring pencils or biros into a pile. Don't rearrange them; you need to play with them in the position they naturally fell into.

- Players then take it in turns to extract a pencil or biro without moving another. If successful, you score points and you get another go. If you move another pen or biro while trying to pick one up, it's the next player's turn.

- Each successfully removed pencil or biro scores the assigned number of points. The person with the most points at the end of the game wins.

Stationery Sculpture

What's the game?

This one will appeal to creatives. It's amazing what contemporary sculpture shapes you can craft from the contents of your stationery cupboard.

What do I need to play it?

Access to a well-stocked stationery cupboard.

How many friends?

However many want to play.

How do I play it?

- Players head to the stationery cupboard and select a pre-agreed number of items.
- You then have fifteen minutes to sculpt and craft at will.
- Best one wins.

Office Treasure Hunt

What's the game?

This takes a little preparation but is worth the invested time. You can employ any sort of clue trail you like, from the technologically advanced to the humble Post-it note. Make sure your treasure is worth hunting for.

What do I need to play it?

Whatever communication devices you want to use to lay your trail: email, Post-it notes, memos, handwritten notes, and so on. Plus some decent treasure to reward the seekers' search.

How many friends?

Works brilliantly for big teams, but equally well for a small gathering. Any number, really, except on your own.

How do I play it?

- First off, plan your treasure hunt route by choosing hiding places and cubby holes that are easily located via an enticing clue, and of course choose the final hiding place of your treasure.
- I'd suggest starting your treasure hunt by email and perhaps directing players to a website that gives a clue as to the location of the next hiding place.
- First to the treasure wins.

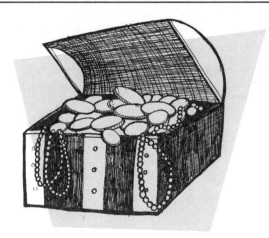

Roller-Chair Rowing

What's the game?

This one became popular after gaining wide viewing figures on YouTube. It's less of a game and more of a stunt, and should get even the grumpiest colleagues giggling behind their computer screens. It requires a bit of practice to nail the synchronicity, but the end effect is well worth the effort.

What do I need to play it?

One of those office chairs on castors for each rower, and something to make a cone-shaped loudspeaker out of.

How many friends?

As many as want to play it, but ideally a number that fits in to a traditional rowing format (two, four or eight), with one person acting as your cox.

How do I play it?

- Agree which rowing format you want to follow and position your chairs facing the same way in a line, with someone acting as your cox facing the way you're rowing.
- Now this takes a bit of practice, but you need to move in time with each other, so as you reach forwards with your arms, you prepare to propel yourselves backwards simultaneously with your chairs.
- Choose the most opportune moment to roll it out, and delight your colleagues by rowing your way through the office.

DVD Discus

What's the game?

Discus rules played with a DVD stolen from the stationery cupboard.

What do I need to play it?

A DVD.

How many friends?

As many as you can rally around to play.

How do I play it?

- First of all, define your throwing area by laying out a circle on the ground using a piece of string.
- Take your DVD discus and position yourself in your throwing area, ensuring there's no one who'll be garrotted, and that your throw will have the opportunity to reach its full potential. You can hold the DVD discus in any way and throw it using any technique. The only rules are that you must not leave the circle before the discus has touched the ground, and you must not touch the ground with any part of the body outside the circle after starting the throw.
- Farthest throw wins.

Corridor Cricket

What's the game?

Many people have laid claim to having invented this game, though I'm sure it was invented in schools across the country as a way of carrying on Cricket practice when it had been rained off.

What do I need to play it?

A standard tennis or cricket bat (or other vaguely bat-shaped object); preferably not too large, to prevent undue damage to the corridor you're playing in. Also any large, solid object to use as the wicket such as a table, box or bin. Oh, and a suitably light ball. A tennis ball is perfect, though this still has the capacity to break a window. If you want to be super safe I'm reliably informed that you can also play with a ball of screwed-up paper.

How many friends?

Ideally played with a bowler, a batsman and a wicket-keeper, with everyone else fielding. Numbers can be increased depending on the size of your corridor.

How do I play it?

- Get yourself set up as for a normal game of Cricket.

- Each player takes it in turn to bat, with the winner being the player with the biggest innings score. For those not familiar with the game, an innings is the period of play for one player. A player's innings ends if they get caught out by another player (the other player catches the ball they've hit) or if they get 'stumped' out (the item that you're using for the wicket gets touched by another player with the ball when the batting player is in mid-run).

- To get started, the bowler bowls towards the batter. If the batter hits the ball they have to run from wicket to wicket.

- You can choose additional scoring mechanics to suit your environment, for example, two points if you hit the ceiling, or four points if you manage to clang the fire extinguisher behind you.

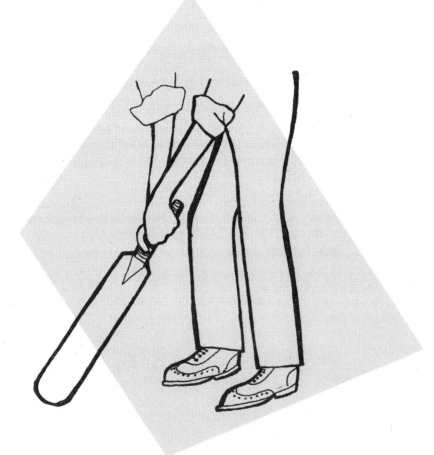

References

1. Healy, Tim, *Life in the Land of the Pharaohs*, Reader's Digest Association, 1995.

2. Ramage, Nancy H. and Ramage, Andrew, *Concise Introduction: Ancient Rome,* British Museum Press, 2008.

3. Yapp, Nick, *Daily Life in the Age of Chivalry*, Reader's Digest Association, 1993.

4. Nicolson, Adam, *Life in the Tudor Age*, Reader's Digest Association, 1995.

5. Goodfellow, Caroline, *How We Played: Games from Childhood Past*, The History Press, 2008.

6. Mangold hurling association, www.mangoldhurling.co.uk.

7. 'Conkers Voted Greatest Playground Game', *Daily Telegraph,* 28 August 2008.

8. 'French Bid to Conker the World', *The Times*, 5 October 2006.

9. Cargill Thompson, Jessica, ed., 'The *Guardian* and *Observer* Guides to Games, Part Two: Party Games', *Guardian*, November 2008.

10. 'Game On', *Guardian Weekend* magazine, 20 December 2008.

Acknowledgements

All of the best games in this book were inspired or created by the wonderfully handsome, erudite and intelligent Barnaby Girling, without whom this wouldn't have happened. Never has this earth seen such a feat of God's creating.

Apologies if I've bored you with waffles of idyllic Devonshire summers but without them and the magic childhood created by my mum and Mary Rose, there wouldn't be anything to put in this book. I would also like to take this opportunity to apologise to my beloved sisters, Suzie and Rachel, for being so bossy and to congratulate them on surviving my childhood gaming dictatorship. Thanks also to my dad and my brother, Michael, for teaching me the art of skimming stones, Pooh Sticks and other essential childhood pleasures.

An abundance of gratitude goes to my very dear friends who have been subjected to and have contributed to many years of incessant and often mandatory organised fun. In height order, they are Arcadia Fletcher, Nix Harding, Elinor Burns, Oriana Elia, Andy Harding, Nick Dugdale-Moore, Olly Gamble and Paddy Cerri.

Special thanks also goes to the creativity and fun-spinning ingenuity of the Australia crew: Amy Sayer, Emily Sayer, Louise Kneafsey, Kate Pryce, Paps Papageorgiou, James Counihan, James Bowden and Ben Parker. And finally the Bristol crew, who were put through what I like to think as the experimental period of my organising fun: Laura Abrahams, Anna Bamford, Beth Gibbon, Emmie Holman, Jane Humphries, Mary Oakes, Meg Connelly, Sonia Taylor-Jones, Molly Mishy May Lewis-Smith, Melissa Radford, Matt Brandon, Richard Taylor-Jones, Penny Lockyer, Dave Karney, Johnno Farrar, Tom Harding (who is also responsible for naming my gaming as 'Organised Fun') and Andy Franks.

Huge thanks to Ronald Somerville, Nick and John Huggins, Brough Girling and Gareth Hawkins for their brilliant contributions and support.

Finally, none of this would of course have happened without Laetitia Rutherford at Mulcahy Conway Associates and the fantastic team at Macmillan, including Jon Butler, Lorraine Green, Sophie Portas, Amy Lines, Rebecca Ikin and Dusty Miller.

Sorry, one more … Otter the dog, for cuddling up to me while writing (just to clarify, that's me writing and not the dog).

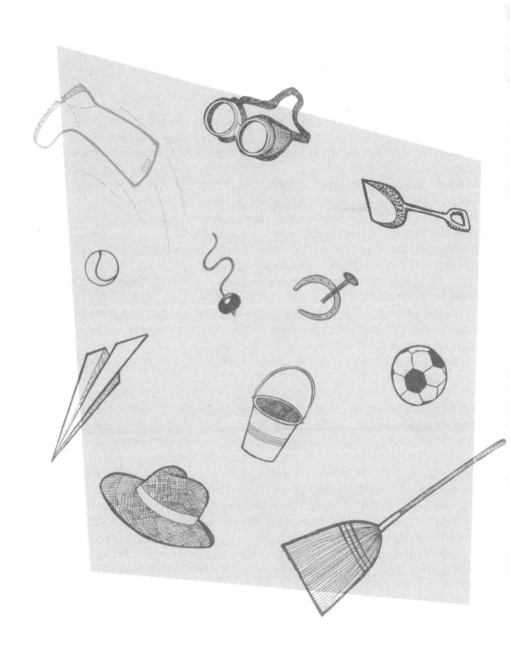